RJ Parker, Ph.D.

MW01076334

TOP **CASES** of The **FBI**

Volume 2

By RJ Parker, Ph.D.

Acknowledgments

Thank you to my editor, proofreaders, and cover artist for your support:

~ **RJ Parker** ~

Aeternum Designs (book cover), Bettye McKee (editor), Lorrie Suzanne Phillippe, Ron Steed, Marlene Fabregas, Robyn MacEachern, Kathi Garcia, Vicky Matson-Carruth, Linda H. Bergeron, Sandra Miller, Laura Swain and audiobook narrator, Steve Carlson

TOP CASES of The FBI
Volume 2

By RJ Parker, Ph.D.

"This is a work of nonfiction. No names have been changed, no characters invented, no events fabricated."

RJ Parker Publishing

ISBN 13: 978-1987902372
ISBN 10: 1987902378

www.RJPARKERPUBLISHING.COM

Published in United States of America

Copyrights

Book Links

AUDIOBOOKS at RJ Parker Publishing
http://rjparkerpublishing.com/audiobooks.html

Collection of CRIMES CANADA books on Amazon.
http://www.crimescanada.com/

TRUE CRIME Books by RJ Parker Publishing on Amazon.
http://rjpp.ca/TRUECRIME-RJPP-BOOKS

ACTION/FICTION Books by Bernard DeLeo on Amazon.
http://bit.ly/BERNARD-DELEO-BOOKS

RJ Parker Publishing

Follow on *BOOKBUB*

Table of Contents

This book is dedicated to my sister, Beverly, on her birthday, Nov 13

"Despite some of these events being acts of terror against U.S. citizens, it is still considered to be war against all of humanity. One drop of blood spilled due to hate is an arrow to the heart that punctures every citizen around the world. We might not be united by race, culture or religion, but events like the ones in this book devastate everyone and certainly brings tears to our eyes and a prayer to our tongues.

Let this serve as a reminder that we need to put aside our differences and unite ourselves against all global threats that reign terror across every street on this earth. Not one country should fight this war alone. We all must play our rightful parts and pray that history should never repeat."

- RJ Parker

Introduction

"The Federal Bureau of Investigation is an intelligence-driven, threat-focused, national security and law enforcement organization— the principal investigative arm of the U.S. Department of Justice and a full member of the U.S. Intelligence Community. It has the authority and responsibility to investigate specific crimes assigned to it and to provide other law enforcement agencies with cooperative services, such as fingerprint identification, laboratory examinations, and training. The FBI also gathers, shares, and analyzes intelligence – both to support its own investigations and those of its partners – to better understand and combat the security threats facing the United States.

"The mission of the the FBI is to protect and defend the United States against terrorist and foreign intelligence threats, to uphold and enforce the criminal laws of the United States, and to provide leadership and criminal justice services to federal, state, municipal, and international agencies and partners. It performs these responsibilities in a way that is responsive to the needs of the public and faithful to the Constitution of the United States. From underworld gangsters to homegrown terrorists, the FBI has tracked down and arrested some of the most notorious criminals in history."

In Volume 2 of Top Cases of The FBI, I selected two famous cases from each of the following criminal categories:

Organized Crime and Gangsters

Counterintelligence/Espionage

Violent Crime/Major Thefts/Bank Robberies

Civil Rights

White Collar Crime

Terrorism

"This is a work of nonfiction. No names have been changed, no characters invented, no events fabricated."

1. Organized Crime and Gangsters

1.1 Joseph (Donnie Brasco) Pistone

Credit of the FBI

Introduction

Donnie Brasco was an alias for undercover FBI agent Joseph Pistone who did a covert operation on the Bonanno crime family and exposed their criminal operations.

Joseph Pistone was born in 1939 in Pennsylvania. He did commendable undercover agent work and earned himself a membership in the Bonanno crime family. However, due to safety issues, the operation had to be eventually shut down, and Joseph Pistone was pulled out.

He graduated from Paterson State College in 1965 with an advanced degree in elementary education civil studies. He worked as a teacher for one year before being appointed to the Office of Naval Intelligence. He was then recruited by the FBI and, after providing his services in the form of different roles, he was transferred to New York in 1974. His ability to drive 18-wheel trucks and bulldozers is what caught the eye of the FBI and helped him land his first undercover operation. This operation required him to infiltrate a gang that was involved in the theft of heavy-duty vehicles and equipment.

He carried out this operation with great success. His infiltration led to the dismantlement of one of the biggest and most profitable theft organizations in the U.S.. More than 30 people were arrested along the Eastern seaboard in February 1976.

The Emergence of Donnie Brasco In Mafia Territory

The infamous Donnie Brasco successfully gained the confidence of New York's notorious Bonanno Mafia family in 1976. He became friends and developed links with several members of the Mafia family who entrusted him with confidential tasks that helped him gather intel about the different criminal operations being carried out by the Bonanno family. This entire undercover assignment lasted for five years, and the superb undercover work done by Pistone led to the apprehension of hundreds of Mafia crime members.

Joseph Pistone was appointed to the New York office in 1974 and was immediately assigned to the truck hijacking squad of the FBI. Mafia families were linked to a number of truck hijacking cases on a daily basis, according to intelligence reports. The FBI devised an operation to take out these Mafia families, and they knew that direct confrontation could result in many casualties; they also knew that these confrontations might not guarantee them success. Considering all these factors, the FBI had to take an alternative route into the secretive world of the Mafia. They provisioned resources and agents for an undercover operation with the alias "SUNA apple" to infiltrate these families. Pistone was given a new identity as a consequence of this. Joseph Pistone was no longer Joseph Pistone. He was now a small-time, successful jewel thief who went around by the name of Donnie Brasco.

Every FBI operation requires preparation, and attention to detail holds paramount importance in these operations. Pistone was sent to school to learn all about precious gems so that he could acquaint himself with the jewel thieving craft. He was given a small apartment in Florida while the rest of his family lived in a different part of the country. He made frequent visits to bars and restaurants which were also a frequent gathering place for Mafia members, and there he met Benjamin "Lefty" Ruggiero for the first time. Ruggiero was a Mafia veteran and had been working for the Mafia for 30 years. He had been linked to the murders of 26 people.

Brasco immediately made an impression on Ruggiero and succeeded in making him his mentor and partner. Ruggiero and Brasco were more than just business partners. Ruggiero was a big brother to Brasco, and Ruggiero took the responsibility of Brasco and gave him his vote of confidence and took him under his wing.

Working as an Undercover Agent

Ruggiero and Brasco joined hands to climb the Mafia ladder together. They would both sit down every day and discuss new and innovative ideas to make more money. Brasco was very cautious and knew exactly what he was doing. He minded his own business and never inquired about other Mafia members. He only worked with people he already knew. He knew that if he asked too many questions, the Mafia could get suspicious and this would blow his cover.

Benjamin "Lefty" Ruggiero joined the Bonanno crime family at a very young age and did his duty as a street soldier diligently. Tony Mirra, who lived in the same complex as Ruggiero, is rumored to be the person who introduced Ruggiero to Joseph Pistone. Ruggiero was well known for extortion, bookmaking, and loansharking and also had a reputation as an enforcer. Being a Mafia gangster is what he was born to be. Brasco once asked Ruggiero why he liked being a gangster, and to this Ruggiero replied by saying that a wise guy can lie, can cheat, can steal, can kill people. He can do anything he wants and no one would say anything about it. Who wouldn't wanna be a wise guy? It was this crooked mentality of his that transformed him into a feared killer. He was given the nickname of

Lefty because he used to throw the dice with his left hand. He was also famous for always bringing two guns with him to a hit. Ruggiero had a habit of gambling that landed him in a lot of debt. His debt amassed to 160,000 dollars by 1977. One of the conditions that the Bonanno family imposed on him to become a made man was to pay his debt, which he did, and eventually became a made man by late 1977.

During his time as an undercover agent, there were times when Brasco was asked to carry out contract killings, and although this placed him in a predicament, he always managed to get himself out of it without drawing suspicion. Sometimes, the FBI staged the killings to aid Pistone.

Brasco's relationship with his wife and his children underwent a serious test during the course of this entire operation. Brasco was given strict orders to not discuss the details of the operation with his family. His family was kept in the dark for their own safety. This created misunderstandings between Brasco and his family

Brasco was an ideal candidate to become an undercover agent for this assignment because of his Sicilian background, fluent Italian and his familiarity with mob culture growing up in the streets of New Jersey. He said that he was in total control when he was carrying out this operation and was well aware of the different rules and regulations of the Mafia system.

In September of 1976, Pistone walked out of the FBI headquarters and didn't return for the next six years. Joseph Pistone was erased from the face of the earth by the FBI, leaving no loose ends. Anyone who came looking for him was told that no one by that name ever worked here. No one knew what happened to him or where he went. He was presumed dead by some people. Pistone's original assignment didn't involve infiltration of the Mafia. His initial goal was to find the people who were involved in the hijacking of heavy-duty trucks and equipment.

During the same time, Pistone was also looking into the Bonanno crime family. Bob Delaney, a police officer under the payroll of the New Jersey state police, was responsible for investigating the organized crime of New Jersey. He maintained affiliations with different crime families for a price and in turn helped them carry out their operations by lowering the pressures of the Union. The two first came across each other through the caporegime of the Colombo crime family. Bob Delaney was unaware at that time that Pistone was actually working undercover.

Pistone became a part of Jilly Greca's

crew which was a part of the Colombo family. Greca's crew was doing truck hijackings on a consistent basis and was also involved in the sale of stolen merchandise. Since only a select few people knew about the true identity of Pistone, the NYPD and FBI listed Pistone as a Mafia gang member, Donnie Brasco.

He eventually made his way into the Bonanno crime family and was able to create close friendships with different members of this notorious Mafia family. His crime affiliates included Anthony Mirra, Dominick Napolitano, and his mentor and father figure Benjamin Ruggiero. Through Ruggiero, Pistone was able to collect substantial information about the Bonanno crime family that would eventually lead to the family's demise. Mafia members were not allowed to talk to non-Mafia members about internal affairs, and this was a strict rule that was imposed on every Mafia member. Pistone and Ruggiero became really close friends with time, and Ruggiero promised to give his life for Brasco if fate asked for such a sacrifice.

Pistone was doing great business for the Bonanno family and was responsible for the successful running of the King's Court Bottle Club which he opened himself. This business venture turned out to be quite lucrative, and there was a time, according to Pistone, when he was just one hit away from becoming a made member of the Bonanno family. He was given orders to kill capo Phillip Giaccone in December of 1981, but the hit was called off on the last minute for some reason. Later, he was hired as a contract killer again to carry out the assassination of Alphonse Indelicato's son, Sonny Red, who was accused of the murder of Indelicato, Giaccone and Dominick Trinchera.

After six years undercover, Pistone's operation was finally shut down. He wanted to carry on with the operation and become a made man. However, he suspected that Napolitano would lie about him and ascertain his loyalty by carrying out a Mafia-ordered hit, and this would deprive the FBI of an opportunity to penetrate the Mafia and humiliate them by revealing that they had been duped by them by introducing an FBI agent into their ranks. Pistone's managers, however, thought it was best to close down the operation before it got out of hand and put Pistone's life in danger. His longtime associates that included Ruggiero and Napolitano came to know about the true identity of Pistone after he was discharged from the FBI.

What Happened after Pistone was pulled out of the undercover operation?

The Mafia family had to hold someone responsible for the humiliation of letting an FBI agent infiltrate their ranks, and Napolitano paid the price for it. He was brutally shot and his hands were cut into pieces by the Mafia family. Anthony Mirra was also killed, and Ruggiero was destined for the same fate, but he was apprehended by the FBI on his way to a meeting. The FBI offered him witness protection, but he declined their offer as he had sworn an oath and he did not want to break it. He stayed true to his word until the very end. Many writers offered him millions of dollars for his story, but he still didn't budge. He was sentenced to 20 years in prison. and he got out at the age of 72. He died soon after in 1994 due to testicular cancer.

Later on, Judy, who was Napolitano's girlfriend, contacted Pistone and told him that Napolitano had no hard feelings for Pistone and he had only love for him. Judy said that she knew that there was something about Pistone that was different from the rest of the gangsters. Pistone was never cut out for the Mafia world, and Judy said all that after finding out that Pistone was an FBI agent.

A $500,000 dollar reward was put on the

head of Pistone and the Bonanno family was kicked out of commission. The FBI had other things in mind. They met with the Mafia bosses in New York and told them about the evidence that had been amassed by Pistone. This evidence led to over 200 indictments and more than 100 convictions of the members of the Mafia. The Bonanno family was left in ruins by Donnie Brasco, but in the end, there was a silver lining in all of this for them. As the Bonanno family was the only family that had lost its privilege to be part of the commission, it was the only family that was not sent to prison.

This was the reason why the Bonanno family was able to keep its leadership intact, and it started to rebuild its reputation from scratch. Gradually, it was able to regain its former glory. The Boss that was the mastermind behind this resurgence was convicted for calling the hit that resulted in the death of Napolitano.

Pistone is still alive and well, and he travels with a fake identity. He also has a license to carry a firearm for the purpose of protection. Pistone is still doing stints as an author and provides his services of consultancy to law enforcement agencies such as Scotland Yard. He has also testified in many high profile cases before the United States Senate, providing his expert opinion on organized crime.

Life after Donnie Brasco

Pistone portrayed the details of his undercover work in his book, Donnie Brasco: My Undercover Life in the Mafia, which was an adaptation of a critically acclaimed film, *Donnie Brasco*, having a star-studded cast which included Johnny Depp as Pistone and Al Pacino as Lefty. Pistone provided his services as a consultant in the film *Donnie Brasco* and made sure that the story of the film didn't stray away from true events that took place in the streets of New Jersey.

A TV show based on Donnie Brasco's life was also created in 2000. The show, which was called Falcone, starred Jason Gedrick as Pistone and, due to some legal reasons, had to change the alias Donnie Brasco to Joe Falcone. Brasco's life also served as the basis for an episode of FBI: The Untold Stories. Pistone himself went on to write a number of books based on his knowledge regarding the Mafia. Some of his books are titled: The Way of the Wiseguy (2004), Donnie Brasco: Unfinished Business (2007), and some fiction books titled Snake Eyes, Mobbed Up, and Deep Cover.

Pistone also wrote a book called The Good Guys with Salvatore Vincent Bonanno, son of Joseph Bonanno. Joseph Bonanno originally did not want Salvatore to become too involved in the Mafia business, but Salvatore disobeyed, and his succession to power and his desire to reach for higher positions led to his family being exiled to Arizona. He ended up producing TV shows and writing books about his family's past (and thus, The Good Guys was born). Pistone also works as an executive producer on many films that are about the Mafia. A documentary series called Mafia's Greatest Hits created by Yesterday had an episode which was based on Pistone.

He also worked on one episode of Secrets of the Dead which was titled Gangland Graveyard. The episode is about the sit-down that happened on May 5, 1981; three Mafia captains were invited under the pretense of having an "administrative meeting" and were then killed by Joseph Massino. Pistone was almost selected to carry out this task, and he holds a substantial amount of knowledge regarding the event, which is why he was consulted while making the episode which finally tells us what happened on May 5, the details of which had hitherto been quite hazy. Much of the show Inside the American Mob was also based on the life of Donnie Brasco. Pistone was interviewed by Rossella Biscotti, an Italian artist, in 2008 in a film titled The Undercover Man. For the film, Biscotti used the film noir approach, submerging the film in black and white and creating a gritty and eerie atmosphere using objects like light bulbs and clocks. Biscotti collected images and documents from the FBI Archives and discussed them with Pistone in the interview which lasted about 30 minutes.

In 2010, a play written by Pistone himself was performed at The Pennsylvania Playhouse. The play, which differed greatly from the 1997 film, starred Pistone's nephew, Joe Pistone II, and explored his relationship with his mentor Ruggiero. While the 1997 film insinuated that Pistone did not want Ruggiero to die, the play, written by the man himself, proved otherwise. While speaking to the audience at The Pennsylvania Playhouse, he said he never cared for Ruggiero. To him, he was nothing more than a killer and he would've killed him without any hesitation or without having a second thought if he could have gotten away with it.

There have been so many adaptations of Pistone's life now that it is hard to tell what is true and what is not. Pistone, however, is always traveling and giving interviews and giving lectures, albeit always under a disguise. He has to use a fake name even when he is in his own neighborhood. And let's face it, it is not easy to go out and give interviews when you have a $500,000 bounty on your head and more than half of the criminals of America are thirsty for your blood, but Pistone has managed to evade the wrath of the Mafia for over 30 years now.

There is another side to this story. Pistone did not go undercover for six years just to end a few Mafia families. He wanted the whole of America to see that these people were not invincible and that they could be put in jail. Thanks to Hollywood, many people at the time were obsessed with gangsters, and they believed that the Mafia was led by people who always spoke in riddles and said intelligent things. Pistone completely destroyed this notion and proved to America that the Mafia consisted of people who do not adhere to a moral code of any sort, people who killed their own. According to one interview, Brasco mentioned that, even though he befriended a lot of people while working with the Mafia, he was always afraid that if anyone found out, they would kill him without any hesitation because these people did not feel bad about killing even their best friends.

According to the same interview, the FBI rewarded Brasco by giving him a medal and 500 dollars. When asked if it was all worth it, he replied it was because he did not do it for the money. He did it because he believed what he did was good for his country and the society he was a part of. The only regret he holds is that he couldn't spend much time with his family.

1.2 Machine Gun Kelly

George Celino 'Kelly' Barnes, or as he was famously known, Machine Gun Kelly, was a bootlegger and a gangster who was active during the Prohibition era in the 1930s. The reason he was called Machine Gun Kelly was because he was very fond of the Thompson submachine gun (or Tommy gun) and he was almost always seen with it. He was arrested on September 26, 1933, for the kidnapping of oil tycoon and businessman Charles Frederick Urschel, and he died of a heart attack while in prison on July 18, 1954.

Credit of the FBI

Introduction

Machine Gun Kelly is considered by many historians as one of the most renowned gangsters of the prohibition era. He was born George Celino Barnes, and he belonged to a wealthy family from Memphis, Tennessee. He was born on July 18, 1895; however, the exact year of his birth varies. Some sources say that he was born in 1897 while according to one of his sons, he was born in 1900 in Chicago. Kelly's childhood was marred by woeful events that had a dire effect on his personality, growing up. He was brought up like all the other kids in Memphis, a place notorious for its Mafia culture.

He wasn't a bright student and performed poorly in educational institutes. In his time at the Mississippi State University studying agriculture in 1917, the highest grade that he was able to attain was a C plus and that was given to him for good physical hygiene. Most of the time, he was caught up in fights and other disagreements with the faculty and staff, and time and time again, his actions proved that a formal education wasn't his cup of tea. His talents were reserved for more diabolical schemes.

However, it should be mentioned that Kelly was not a gangster in the truest sense. His famous nickname that he got from the submachine gun he always carried with him was just that. A nickname. He was never seen shooting anyone with the Thompson submachine gun, and in all his life as a gangster, he never killed a single person. In fact, when Kelly kidnapped a banker in 1932, he demanded him to pay $50,000 in ransom but decided to let him go after two days without even getting the money. In the months that followed, Kelly and his men would regularly call the banker and ask him to pay the money, but they soon stopped calling and did not bother the man again.

His Entry into the World of Crime

During his abysmal academic time in the Mississippi State University, he met a woman named Geneva Ramsey. Kelly gave in to Geneva's charms and fell head over heels in love with her and made an abrupt and absurd decision to marry her and leave school. Kelly had two children with Geneva and worked as a cab driver to provide for his family. He was working day and night, but he was still not able to earn much and this frustrated him sorely. This menial job as a cab driver was not enough to support his family and provide food and other basic necessities to his children and wife. Kelly had to make a decision. He left his job as a cab driver to find a career in other promising avenues. The stress and the disappointment at such an immature age of 19 caused strife within the family which resulted in separation from his wife. According to his wife, the reason she left him was because he was "running in bad company". He was completely broke and desperate to earn a livelihood to make ends meet. It was during this time that he started his career as a bootlegger, and he got a stable income as well as notoriety from this new venture.

This notoriety, however, had a downside to it as well. He was often on the police radar because of it and was arrested several times in the underground for illegal trafficking. By this time, Kelly had gotten himself a new girlfriend. He decided to move away with her from Memphis and head west. In order to not give a bad name to his revered family back in Memphis, he adopted a new alias, George R. Kelly. In this new place, Kelly's fortunes didn't plummet. He continued his business with great success and made a name for himself in the underground. By 1927, he had already been arrested several times by the police and had spent a lot of time behind prison walls. He was now feared as a seasoned gangster. In 1928, he was indicted on charges of contraband and sentenced to three years in jail when he was apprehended smuggling liquor to an Indian reservation. However, his luck soon ran out and he was arrested and locked up in a prison in northeast Kansas.

During his time in prison, he befriended many strange and unusual-looking people. He started talking to people who robbed banks for a living and he felt inspired to do the same once he got out of prison. He carried out many heists after leaving prison and made a name for himself through this. Some of the places where he was known to rob banks were Texas, Washington, Mississippi, Minnesota, and Iowa. It was during this time he made a plan to kidnap the banker whom he eventually let go without taking any money. He was now finally starting to become known throughout America.

Prohibition Era

In 1919, The National Prohibition Act was passed in America which allowed the legislation to pass the 18th Amendment. The 18th Amendment banned the transportation, sale, and production of alcohol. The Jazz Age (1920s) produced people who were not happy with the Eighteenth Amendment, and they were willing to get their alcohol through illegal means. This resulted in many people taking the law in their own hands and forming gangs and smuggling alcohol into the United States from Canada and other countries.

This entire period was infested with criminal activities. The crime rate in America increased and new gangsters were popping up on the map every day. The American government had hoped to reduce the crime rate with the Eighteenth Amendment, but instead, exactly the opposite happened and the crime rate doubled. One of the most famous gangsters during the Prohibition Era was perhaps Alphonse "Scarface" Capone, who operated in Chicago. Capone made over $60 million every year by selling beer. Many gangsters saw the 18th Amendment as an easy way to make money as Prohibition helped alcohol find its way into the Black Market.

Machine Gun Kelly belonged to a good, well-to-do family, but his job as a cab driver wasn't enough to put food on the table, and the divorce from his wife Geneva drove him to despair. He saw bootlegging as a way out of his misery and poverty. Being a gangster wasn't very hard during the Prohibition Era, and bribing police officers to escape prison was a very common thing among gangsters at the time. Kelly was not cut out for the gangster life, as evidenced by the incompetent behavior he exhibited when he kidnapped Urschel, but, driven by despair, he took the opportunity and decided to get into the business of bootlegging and eventually bank robberies and kidnappings. He saw that this was the only way he could make some money.

Kelly's Further Descent into the World of Crime

After serving time at Leavenworth (in northeast Kansas), Kelly was thrown into another prison in New Mexico in 1929. When he got out, he moved to Oklahoma City and started working with Steve Anderson, a bootlegger like himself. This was where he met his new girlfriend, Kathryn Thorne (later Kathryn Kelly). Kathryn worked for Steve Anderson and, just like George Kelly, she was a criminal too. In fact, various members of her family were known criminals too and she had been to prison many times for her crimes which included prostitution and robberies. Kathryn was a very dangerous person, and it seemed that everyone around her was, in a way, cursed. She had married twice, and her second husband was shot dead by someone. While his death was ruled a suicide, the actual reason was much sinister. It was suspected that it was Kathryn herself who had murdered her husband.

Nevertheless, Kathryn and George fell in

love and they married in 1930 in Minneapolis. It was Kathryn who gifted George the weapon that gave him the nickname "Machine Gun Kelly". It is now believed that it was Kathryn who popularized the nickname among other criminals. She would urge George to practice with the gun she gifted him and later show the gun cartridges to her associates at clubs and bars, saying they were souvenirs from "Machine Gun" Kelly. Kathryn remained George's partner in crime until he was caught and sent to prison. She helped him in a number of robberies George carried out in Mississippi and Texas. It did not take George Kelly long to establish a name for himself in the crime world, and the FBI soon had Wanted Posters of him all over America. The posters called him "Expert Machine Gunner".

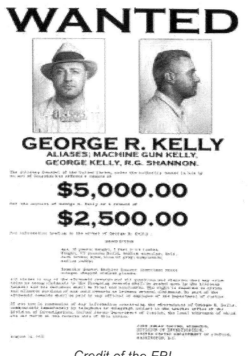

Credit of the FBI

The Famous Kidnapping

George soon realized that he was not making enough money with just robberies and bootlegging. He knew that he was capable of much more. So, with the help of his wife, Kathryn Kelly, he started formulating a plan to kidnap the rich oil tycoon and businessman, Charles Frederick Urschel. But Kelly knew that he could not do it alone, so he hired two other men. On July 22, 1933, together with his wife and the two men, he broke into Urschel's house in Oklahoma City. When they entered into the house, Mr. and Mrs. Urschel, along with Mr. and Mrs. Jarret, were playing a card game of bridge. Kelly shouted that he would "blow everyone's head off" and decided to kidnap both Urschel and Jarret.

At first, Kelly and his fellow men could not figure out which one of the two men was Urschel and, because they were not cooperating, Kelly started searching for their IDs. When they finally found Jarret's ID and learned who he was, they decided to take $51 from his wallet and then let him go. Then they took Urschel to a farm in Texas and started demanding money. They asked for a ransom of $200,000.

Thanks to Urschel's wife who had called John Edgar Hoover, the director of the FBI, as soon as the gangsters had left the premises of their house, Special Agents reached Oklahoma City as soon as possible and began their investigation. The ineptitude of the whole crime can be understood by how Kelly simply released Urschel's friend Jarret after taking $51 from his wallet. When Kelly let him go, he told him not to tell anyone where they were headed. When the FBI questioned Jarrett, he told them that the kidnappers went south after letting him go.

Kelly and his accomplices became even more famous than they already were because of this event, and the FBI soon had people calling them and sending them anonymous letters, some of them giving valuable information as to the whereabouts of the kidnappers. Urschel had a friend in Tulsa, Oklahoma, named J. G. Catlett who received a letter written by Urschel that asked him to act as an intermediary for his release. The letter also said that Catlett had to go to Oklahoma City immediately and that he had to refrain from communicating by telephone. Mr. Catlett received another letter that talked about the ransom money and asked Catlett to publish the following ad:

"FOR SALE --- 160 Acres Land, good five room house, deep well. Also Cows, Tools, Tractor, Corn, and Hay. $3750.00 for quick sale. TERMS. Box # ___ "

In the letter, it was also mentioned that if Catlett tried to deceive or trick the kidnappers, then he would only find the remains of Urschel. The kidnappers set July 29th, 1933, as the date of the meeting.

When the FBI got their hands on the letter, they did not try to identify the writer, but they immediately got down to making arrangements for the meeting. $200,000 in $20 notes were arranged and their serial numbers were written down. To make sure that nothing went wrong, they took another bag and filled it with old magazines. Catlett was sent with a Mr. E. E. Kirkpatrick to ensure his safety. On the first day, Kirkpatrick and Catlett waited for the kidnappers, but they never showed up.

Later that day, a telegram was sent to Kirkpatrick anonymously from Tulsa, Oklahoma, which said that the kidnappers could not arrive at the destination due to some "unavoidable incident". Next day, on July 30, the kidnappers called Kirkpatrick and told him to meet them at LaSalle Hotel. Kirkpatrick asked them if he could bring a friend, but they refused and told him that he was to come alone. Kirkpatrick arrived at the hotel with the money at 6 p.m. One of the kidnappers met him, took the money, and told him to go back to his hotel and they would return Urschel after they inspected the money.

After being held captive for nine days, Urschel was finally released and he came home on July 31st around 11:30 pm. His time with the kidnappers had left him distraught. He said he had not been able to sleep while he was with them. The FBI decided not to disturb him until he himself was willing to talk to them and tell them where the kidnappers were.

After some days, when he had picked up his strength, he went to the FBI himself where he was interviewed by special agents. Urschel was surprisingly very precise about all the details he gave to the FBI regarding the kidnappers. He told the FBI everything, from the behavior and the conversations of the kidnappers to actions taken by himself. Urschel gave the FBI a detailed statement of everything that happened after he was kidnapped. Urschel had been handcuffed to a chair and was asked if he knew anyone in Tulsa, Oklahoma, who could be trusted to bring them the money. He gave them the name of Catlett and then the kidnappers asked him to write Catlett a letter.

The Investigation and Arrest

At first, the FBI did not go after the kidnappers because their first priority was saving Urschel. But after Urschel was safe, the FBI started looking more deeply into the case. It had only been two days since Urschel was kidnapped and the FBI had already gotten a clue as to who the kidnappers were. They had obtained evidence that suggested that George and Kathryn Kelly were behind the kidnapping.

Nevertheless, a proper investigation was started and the FBI began looking into the past of these two individuals. The FBI learned that

George Kelly was spending more money than he could have earned and that he had no means through which he could have earned that much money unless he was involved in something illegal. They later found out that he was a bootlegger and had been to prison many times. They also investigated Kelly's wife and found out that it was she who had encouraged George to become more active in bank robberies and kidnappings.

During the interview with Mr. Urschel, he told the special agents that he could hear a plane fly over the place where he was being held almost every day around 10 a.m. The only day when he didn't hear the plane was when it was raining. This information proved to be very useful in locating the kidnappers. The FBI consulted various people to learn about the weather conditions of the places in Oklahoma and surrounding areas and also the airplane schedules.

Their investigation led them to Paradise, Texas, where Kathryn Kelly's mother lived. The house of Kathryn's mother was located, and a special agent went there to take a look. The agent realized that the house looked exactly like the area Urschel had described in his statement. He also learned that George and Kathryn Kelly had been spotted near the house.

The FBI carried out a raid on the house of Kathryn's mother on August 12. Harvey J. Bailey, a criminal who had been responsible for killing three police officers and an FBI special agent, was arrested. Kathryn's mother, Ora L. Shannon, was taken into custody along with her husband, R. G. Shannon, and son, Armon Shannon. When Urschel was shown the house, he recognized it at once as the place where he was taken by his kidnappers. He also revealed that it was Ora's husband, R. G. Shannon, and his son Armon who had stood guard over him. The Shannons confirmed this. All of the people who worked with George and Kathryn Kelly were soon arrested and were sent to prison.

Further investigation revealed that the Kellys were hiding at a residence at Memphis. Special agents were sent there immediately who carried out a raid. Both George and Kathryn Kelly were found there without any weapons. George Kelly shouted the now famous words "Don't shoot, G-Men!" before he surrendered to the special agents. The word "G-Men" had been used before, but it wasn't until Machine Gun Kelly uttered them that the usage of the word started gaining prominence. The Kellys were arrested on October 12th, 1933, and were sentenced to life imprisonment.

Some part of the ransom money was found at a ranch owned by Cassey Earl

Coleman on September 27. Coleman was also sent to prison for conspiring with a fugitive. All other people who helped the Kellys in their plan were soon located and arrested. George Kelly died of a heart attack at Leavenworth in 1954. His wife, Kathryn Kelly, who was being held in a prison in Cincinnati, was released in 1958, four years after her husband's death. And thus, the legend of "Machine Gun" Kelly finally came to an end.

2. Counterintelligence and Espionage

2.1 Robert Hanssen - American Traitor

Credit of the FBI

Introduction

Robert Philip Hanssen was a U.S. FBI agent who was indicted for spying and charged with committing espionage against the mighty United States. He is still currently serving his life sentence in ADX Florence prison. Hanssen was working against the U.S. with Soviet and Russian intelligence services and fed them classified information that revealed secrets about U.S. security, identities of spies working in the Soviet, and also damaging and endangering secrets about U.S. nuclear operations as well as a secret U.S. lair and tunnel in Washington, under the Soviet Embassy.

History

Now, before we get into juicier details, we must first talk about the origins and the life history of this man. Perhaps, somewhere along the way, we may begin to understand the motivation behind such life-altering actions of this U.S. traitor. Or maybe perhaps, we won't.

Robert Hanssen was born in 1944 in Chicago, Illinois, and was a son to a police officer who was emotionally abusive to Hanssen. Perhaps, instead of looking up to his father as a role model and wanting to make him proud, he wanted to corrode everything his father worked hard for. Resentment can cause bitter apples to grow, and a fuel for revenge can cost a man his life as well his morals, though we may never know this for sure. This is merely a speculation.

Hanssen studied from William Howard Taft High School and then went to Knox College where he earned a Bachelor's degree in chemistry. (Perhaps he may have been better off making crystal meth in an episode of Breaking Bad rather than being a bad cop in some other TV show because, well, that never ends well.)

Before he started working for the FBI, Hanssen achieved many things. But firstly, he was rejected for the position as a cryptographer for the National Security Agency (NSA) due to financial cutbacks (this was perhaps considered an achievement for the NSA). Then he studied in a dental college where he met the love of his life, Bernadette Wauck, whom he married in 1968. After three years of staring at teeth, he changed his career path and received an MBA degree, after which he worked for an accounting firm. Then he quit after a year to join the forces of the Chicago Police Department where he worked as an Internal Affairs Investigator. He joined the FBI in early 1976. (Wrong move, Hanssen.)

Now, after he married his wife, he became influenced by his wife's Catholicism and hence converted his ideologies and got involved in Opus Dei, a conservative, traditional Catholic organization.

Life as an FBI agent and a snitch

Hanssen, a father of three, got promoted as a special agent on January 12, 1976, whereupon he was transferred to Indiana. And then again in 1978, he, along with his family, moved to New York City. I guess the tremors of trouble began a year later when he was moved in the counter-intelligence department and was made to compose a database on Soviet Intelligence for the FBI.

Now just after three years of working as a special agent, Hanssen began showing his true colours when he approached Soviet GRU (Glavnoye Razvedyvatel'noye Upravleniye, the Russian armed forces) and offered to work for them. (Pawn moves forward on the chess board.) Now, to be clear, this move did not stem from political motivation; rather his pockets were not warm enough. In other words, Hanssen was a greedy snitch. This was revealed after he was caught. Let's give him credit for being honest at least.

Now during his first shenanigan, he made an exchange for information on suspected Soviet agents and bugging schemes of the FBI. The most lethal outcome of the consequence of his actions was, perhaps, against Dmitri Polyakov. Dmitri Polyakov worked as a CIA informant, transferring information to the American intelligence when he got promoted as a General in the Soviet Army. (Snitches, snitches everywhere.) No action was taken against Dmitri (maybe the Russians thought he was too pretty to kill) until he was caught for the second time. Then the poor lad was executed. (What was he thinking, he's not that pretty now.)

Okay, so the blame fell on Aldrich Ames, another snitch of CIA, but the real culprit was (drum roll) our man, Robert Hanssen. This was revealed when Hanssen was caught in 2001.

Further Shenanigans

Once a domino falls, you know what happens next. The other dominoes also fall. Hence once Hanssen got started, he must have thought, why stop now? However, in 1980 he came clean to his wife and told her the truth after he was caught with some suspicious-looking material. He admitted about his illegal affair with the Soviets but told her it was just worthless information (I think Dmitri would beg to differ, Hanssen.) His wife urged him to stop (and a real man never says no) and so he promised to do so and confessed to a priest who told him to donate the tainted money. But spying was a drug and he was addicted. He relapsed and continued his espionage in 1985. In 1981, he was transferred to Washington, D.C., where he had access to information on various FBI operations. The activities included wiretapping and surveillance for which Hanssen was responsible. As a man of many talents, he became well-known for being a computer geek.

So, three years later, he was moved to Soviets Analytical Unit where the work he was assigned pertained to studying, recognizing and arresting Soviet spies in the U.S. So, the task was mainly to determine whether the Soviet snitches were triple agents or were genuinely working in favor of the U.S.

In 1985, he was transferred once again to New York City in field offices where he worked in counter intelligence. On a trip back to Washington, he resumed his spy work when he communicated with the Komitet Gosudarstvennoy Bezopasnosti, translated in English as Committee for State Security (KGB) via anonymous letter, once again asking for a job of exchanging his services for a mere $100,000. This letter was the beginning of Hanssen's infiltration with the KGB.

He gave KGB three names of the Soviet traitors, Boris Yuzhin, Valery Martynov and Sergei Motorin who were caught, oblivious of the fact that Aldrich Ames had already revealed the names before him. Marty and Moto were put to eternal sleep with bullets in their heads while Boris was imprisoned.

Again, no one suspected Hanssen of betrayal because Ames was blamed.

In 1987, Hanssen was assigned to find the spy who revealed those names. In other terms, himself. During this course of study, he obviously made sure his track was crystal clean but also turned over the study itself and FBI Soviet moles to the KGB in 1988. During the same year, Hanssen was reported for a security breach, where he slipped some secret info to a Soviet defector, although no action was taken against him.

In 1989, during an investigation of a State Department official named Felix Bloch, suspected for espionage, Hanssen sabotaged the case by warning KGB of the ongoing investigation. Obviously, this caused KGB to sever ties with the man, and hence the FBI could find no proof of Bloch's activities, although he was sacked. Life is unfair it may seem, because Hanssen continued his way up toward the hierarchy and eventually worked in senior counterintelligence roles. But it was this last event that caused the FBI to ponder over how KGB found out about Bloch's investigation, and so their search came to an end when the road led directly to Hanssen.

Now, we move forward to more juicier details on what Hanssen exposed to the Russians. Not only did Hanssen hand over information on MASINT (Measure and Signature Intelligence), which included radars, spy satellites and signal intercepts as well as lists of U.S. double agents, and also revealed to them about the tunnel dug underneath the Soviet embassy, constructed in 1977, originally intended for spying and eavesdropping but was not used because of the fear of getting caught (hah, sissies). In return Hanssen received a payment of $55,000 USD. (At least they paid good, eh?)

Now sometime during the year of 1990, a former FBI employee (and Hanssen's brother-in-law) reported to the FBI that Hanssen should be investigated for espionage. This seed of suspicion was sowed by Bonnie's sister, Bernadette, who saw a stack of money sitting carelessly on his dresser. (She probably knew the FBI doesn't pay that well). Unfortunately, no action was taken against him. Hanssen continued his way down the slippery slope.

After the collapse and downfall of the Soviet Union in 1991, Hanssen stopped his spy work for fear of getting caught. Though when the Russian Federation resurrected the ashes of the fallen USSR spy agencies, Hanssen made the bold move of meeting the GRU, for whom he used to work but had not contacted for at least 10 years. He went to a GRU officer in person, using the pseudonym of Ramon Garcia, under the false pretense of being a disaffected FBI agent and offering his services. But the Russians, believing him to be a triple agent, reported "Ramon Garcia" to the FBI. Again, Hanssen got lucky because the Bureau's investigation in this matter did not progress.

During the further chain of events,

Hanssen printed out a classified document by hacking the computer of an FBI agent named Ray Mislock and then proceeded to tell him, "You didn't believe me that the system was insecure." Though this triggered an investigation, Mislock came to the conclusion that this document was merely made up to cover his tracks because Hanssen was looking for info as to whether he was being investigated for espionage. The officials inferred that this was simply a demonstration of flaws in the FBI's security system.

Another FBI agent, a convicted mole, told the FBI that he suspected Hanssen of espionage, but his superiors turned a blind eye towards the accusation.

Now following an IT failure, some personnel from National Security Division investigated Hanssen's computer and found a hacking attempt by a password-cracking program installed in the computer which Hanssen covered up by telling them it was for connecting his computer to a color printer which required an administrative password. He was once again believed but was given a warning. (So scary.)

Hanssen, being desperate, scoured case records using his own name in the FBI search engines to see whether he was being investigated for espionage. Satisfied, he began his spy work again after eight years and became involved with SVR, Russia's foreign intelligence service, in 1999.

Fall of Hanssen

Following the arrest of Aldrich Ames in 1994, many of the suspicious activities, such as the execution of Martynov and Motorin, were explained. However, many matters were unresolved, such as who tipped off the KGB during Bloch's investigation and the unexplained revelation of the secret tunnel. Ames was not accused of this because he was in Rome during Bloch's investigations.

So, the CIA and FBI joined forces and conducted a mole investigation; this operation was code named "Graysuit". (Picture men in black suits scratching their heads, looking all confused). CIA agent Harold James Nicholson was revealed as a spy during this investigation, but Robert Hanssen (lucky lad) dodged the suspicious glares of the officials again. Following the false accusation of an FBI agent named Kelley, who was involved in Bloch's investigation, the FBI decided to take a different approach. The FBI did not find any evidence on Kelley, and though he was innocent but not proven so until Hanssen's arrest, Kelley was placed on leave.

The collapse of Hanssen's secret spy reign began in 2000. The FBI paid US$7million to a former KGB agent to reveal the identity of the mole. This was to be done by acquiring a file from the SVR headquarters. This Russian and his family were protected by the U.S. and given new identities. Sometime in November of 2000, the FBI got their hands on the file. This file consisted of notes and audio tapes. The audio tape was a record of conversations between an FBI mole and a KGB agent. Michael Waguespack knew the voice but couldn't place it with a face, and it wasn't until they scoured the notes and found a General George S. Patton quote about "a purple pissing Japanese" that the FBI analyst remembered Hanssen quoting that very same thing. (Pro tip for spies: never quote something twice.) The voice was recognized and fingerprints on a trash bag confirmed that Hanssen was, indeed, the spy.

Hanssen was now closely but secretly under surveillance which revealed that Hanssen was still in contact with the Russians. (Maybe Hanssen did it for free Vodka?) For close supervision and so that Hanssen did not have access to more sensitive information, he was promoted to supervise computer security. Hanssen was assigned an assistant (who was obviously an FBI agent secretly spying on the spy). Eric O'Neil found that Hanssen was using a Palm III PDA to store his information. Once this was deciphered and decrypted, the FBI had hard proof.

Robert Hanssen was anything but an idiot. He knew something was up because he was assigned the task of staring at computer monitors. It was also reported that he had asked his friend at a computer technology firm if he could work for them. Additionally, he suspected his car was bugged because his car radio was making strange noises. In a letter to the Russians found after his capture, he had written that the "sleeping tiger had been aroused".

Okay, so he was an idiot because, despite his suspicion, he continued on his missionary espionage.

This is how and when things went downhill. On February 18, 2001, Hanssen dropped his friend at the airport and drove to Foxstone Park in Virginia. There, he signaled his fellow Russians that new information was available. The signal was a white tape on the park sign. Then Hansen took a sealed garbage bag and taped it under a wooden footbridge over a creek.

Obviously, this was a highly dubious act and one which invoked the arrest. He was caught during the act, red handed, and was smug enough to say, "What took you so long?" The FBI waited around for two days to see whether the Russians would show, and when they didn't, the arrest of Robert Hanssen was formally declared on February20, 2001.

Arrest and Punishment

Hanssen was able to get a plea bargain as he promised cooperation with authorities and in this way, he avoided a death penalty. On July 6, 2001, he pleaded guilty on all 15 charges of espionage (Cue a long whistle.) The following year on May 10, he was sentenced to 15 consecutive life sentences which he is still serving, without the opportunity of release on parole. (No surprise here.) His new home is the supermax prison close to Florence, Colorado, where he shares his spy stories with infamous fellow prison inmates such as Unabomber Ted Kaczynski and Ramzi Yousef.

Ramon Garcia

Apart from approaching the GRU officer in person, Hanssen was smart enough to never meet his Russian friends in person and used an alias, "Ramon Garcia". The exchange of information and money was done through a dead drop system, where the packages were left in public places. He was also smart enough to reject places that his handler, Viktor Cherkashin, suggested.

A coding system was devised for timings of exchange. Six was added to the actual time and date.

Hanssen's Fame

Apparently, Hanssen became famous enough to be written about. There are two entire chapters in a book called "The Secrets of the FBI" dedicated to him. These chapters are titled "Catching Hanssen" and "Breach". (I think Practice What You Breach would've been a witty title.)

Not only a book, a movie was also made on him, and these chains of events were scarcely portrayed in this movie called Breach. Have these people considered that making a movie on such people aids the rise of criminal activities because media plays a role in making them famous?

Again, a documentary titled Superspy: The Man Who Betrayed the West was dedicated towards Hanssen's capture. Master spy: The Robert Hanssen story is again made on this guy. I mean, this man is depicted so much on media. Hello? Is he a traitor or a hero? Make up your mind and stop honoring Hanssen. Last time I checked, he's the reason many of the U.S. spies were executed. Well, Hanssen was allowed to watch this movie from prison, but he switched it off, angered by it. (Yes, feed his ego. Great move guys.)

He was also a character in Dan Brown's book "The Da Vinci Code" somewhere in chapter 5, as an FBI spy and Opus Dei member. Lastly, David Wise wrote a book in 2002 called Spy: The Inside Story of How FBI's Robert Hanssen Betrayed America in which the author tells all the things which I have written above, but in greater detail.

Though it took nearly 15 years to find the spy who worked against the U.S. and collaborated with the Russians, they still closed one of the deadliest cases of espionage. And the worst part is Robert Hanssen did it for money. How greedy could one be that he sells his country for money? Did he feel no sentiment for the land he grew up on? I guess not. And that is what makes us question how many people are alive right now with crooked morals and a half teaspoon of humanity in them.

An FBI agent is sworn to protect and is bound by an oath that he must honor until his dying breath. Instead Robert Hanssen continuously ignored the weight of responsibility caused by uttering mere words and led such a life that his name leaves a bitter taste in our mouths. Someone who betrays his country does not belong anywhere, but that is my belief. Right now, the fact that he is serving 23 hours a day in solitary confinement provides us with comfort that perhaps justice is served. He may now spy for his inmate friends, who had what for breakfast.

Credit of the FBI

2.2 Year of the Spy 1985

Credit of the FBI

Jonathan Pollard

Jonathan Pollard and Ronald Pelton, the infamous spies from the year of spies 1985, were recently released on parole. This has opened quite a few ears in the media. Their liberation after serving a tedious sentence of thirty years has drawn a lot of attention in different spheres. The year 1985 holds paramount importance in the history of reputable law enforcement agencies such as the FBI, KGB, etc. Many attempts were made to halt espionage operations during the Cold War, and these persistent attempts did come to fruition as many spies were apprehended and locked up.

Credit of the FBI

Ronald Pelton

Nineteen eighty-five was the year of surprising defections of notable intelligence officers. Some of the names that defected from the East to the West and West to the East include KGB London Station Chief Oleg Gordievsky, renowned and revered intelligence officer Hans-Joachim Tiedge, and KGB officer Vitaly Yurchenko who changed his allegiance from the Soviet Union to the United States. All these defections had underlying lurid details that were later unveiled to the public.

During these times, eight American citizens who betrayed the country were convicted on account of treason because they were themselves betrayed by the people they were working for. What do you expect when you decide to set your feet in a world of deception and lies?

Most of the spies worked for the Russian intelligence agency, the KGB, but there were spies who had sworn their loyalties to countries other than the Soviet Union. Pollard was working for Israel, CIA operative Marie Scranage was working under the command of Ghanian authorities. The Ghanian operatives employed a special investigative strategy known as the honey trap in which they used their sexual allure to advocate their spy activities. This honey trap was used to cast a seductive spell on Marie Scranage to extract confidential information out of her.

Ronald Pelton and Vitaly Yurchenko

Before being hired by the NSA, Ronald Pelton provided his services as a voice intercept specialist in the U.S. Air force. During his time in the U.S. Air Force, he learned the Russian language and was assigned to a post in Peshawar, Pakistan. After that stint of 15 months, his expertise was needed elsewhere and he was picked up by the NSA where he served for many years before he decided to retire from the agency.

As a string of defections and treachery continued to be disclosed, Ronald Pelton, who was a retired NSA analyst and had an insatiable thirst for money and other heinous motives, was exposed by the KGB defector Vitaly Yurchenko. Yurchenko had become quite cooperative after changing sides and was desperate to help his new masters in order to earn some kind of repentance on his part. That is why he was more than willing to hand out information that he had gathered during his time as a spy. Pelton went bankrupt and decided to resign from the NSA shortly after that. Pelton was hesitant to talk about his work at the NSA at first, but this all changed when he stepped into the Russian embassy in Washington, D.C., in January of 1980.

Due to the overwhelming financial pressure on his shoulders, he decided to sell highly classified information to the Soviet authorities in return for a hefty sum. He didn't bring documents along with him, but he had worked as a loyal secrecy worker for so long in the NSA that he had familiarized himself with many secrets of the agency.

Pelton visited Vienna in 1980 and 1983 and was invited to the Soviet Ambassador's house in Austria. He participated in long sessions with high-ranking Russian officials there that sometimes went on for more than eight hours. Pelton had worked for a long time in the NSA, and he had amassed valuable secrets during that time. The Soviets took full advantage of that fact and hired Pelton as an intelligence consultant after he left the NSA. Pelton was careful; he didn't provide any tangible evidence in the form of documents or classified files to the Russians and only relied on his recollections in the NSA to give information to the Russians. He was paid quite a sum for his services. Some reports suggest that the Russians paid him a whopping $37,000 dollars in exchange for the information.

The Ivy Bells operation that was being carried out to tap Soviet underwater military communications was also revealed by Pelton. The amount of information that Pelton had stored in his mind while working in the NSA was dumbfounding and was enough to cause severe damage to the U.S. Government, and the Russian intelligence agencies were well aware of that.

The Walker Spy Ring

A member of the U.S. intelligence who revealed confidential information to foreign governments made headlines in the newspapers in 1985. Why did he do this? Why do humans do most of these things? They do it for money. The Navy was shocked when one of their own, John Walker, was caught by the police on charges of espionage and treason. He was not the only one who was involved in these treacherous covert operations. The whole Walker Spy Ring which included John Walker's brother Arthur, his son Michael, and Jerry Whitworth, who was also a former shipmate, were also exposed. Michael was the only member of the ring who was lucky enough to be released from federal prison. His father and uncle shared a horrendous fate and met their ends in the federal prison, as we know that not everyone has it in him to survive in a federal prison.

The Walker Spy Ring was getting orders from the Soviet Union, China, and Cuba. However, the real shock came when the U.S. authorities found out that a U.S. official was involved in espionage for an ally country, Israel. This news sent shock waves across the entire intelligence world of the United States.

Jonathan Pollard

The US wasn't expecting this from Israel due to the fact that the U.S. was one of the first countries that accepted the sovereignty of Israel as a new state in 1948. The U.S. and Israel have very firm ties and a relationship that spans over several decades. They have worked together and shared intelligence even though they have undergone periods of severe political tension. One such example of political tension is when the Israeli military attacked the USS Liberty AGTR-6 in the Mediterranean Sea off the coast of Israel.

Jonathan Pollard is one of the most highlighted spies in the history of the U.S. He left some loose ends while working as an intelligence analyst at the Naval Investigative Service's Anti-Terrorism Analysis Center and paid the price for it. His slight carelessness and lack of attention to detail to his real job, i.e., espionage got him arrested. His wife Anne Henderson was also apprehended by the police and interrogated by the FBI. Pollard made a futile attempt to gain entry into the Israeli Embassy and get citizenship after being investigated by the FBI and the Naval Investigative Service. The Israeli authorities refuted all claims that Pollard was working for them for many years. He delivered confidential documents to the Israeli Intelligence Agency, Lishka le-Kishrei Mada (LAKAM) through an Israeli correspondent. Finally, in 1998, Israel finally admitted that Pollard was, in fact, working for them as a spy and that he provided intelligence reports to Israeli agents. Israel made many attempts to get Jonathan Pollard out of American custody and to grant him asylum by lobbying many U.S. Presidents, and they succeeded when he was granted Israeli citizenship in 1996.

Pollard argued that the reason he indulged in espionage operations for Israel was because America didn't provide intelligence reports on some countries that were deemed as a common threat. So, he had to infiltrate the Naval Intelligence in order to get tangible intelligence reports on countries such as the United Arab Emirates (UAE) and Pakistan. According to him, that was his motive behind his treasonous actions.

Pollard also told the authorities that he betrayed the United States because he had sworn allegiance to Israel. He stated that he did it for ideological reasons and his inherent and deep-rooted love for Israel. His desire to do something for his country can be traced back to his college days. Pollard believed that he was already working for the Mossad in his college days.

Pollard wasn't taken to trial in front of a U.S. attorney. Instead, the whole thing was settled in the form of a plea bargain. Pollard confessed to his crimes and a sentence was agreed upon behind closed doors. Pollard had to make this sacrifice and accept the length of the sentence given to him so that his wife Anne Henderson could get a shorter sentence in return for his sacrifice.

Pollard, though, didn't hand out U.S. information to Israel, but his betrayal led to the attack on a Palestine Liberation Organization (PLO) office in Tunisia. Israel knew about U.S. assets and methods through Pollard. They passed on this confidential information to a third country, South Africa, which then attacked Tunisia, a U.S. ally.

Sharon Scranage

Sharon Marie Scranage, a CIA operative, got involved in a romantic relationship with Michael Soussoudis. They used this honey trap to get their hands on highly classified information. The affair went on for almost 18 months, and there is no blatant evidence that points to the fact that the CIA commanded Scranage to get romantically involved with Michael Soussoudis. The real reason behind Scranage's involvement is still unknown. A security officer first noticed a picture on Scranage's mirror when he was invited to her home for dinner. The picture depicted a shirtless Soussoudis. After Scranage returned to the U.S. from her assigned mission, she failed a polygraph test which led to further suspicion. She was investigated by the CIA shortly after that, and this led the CIA to believe that Scranage had, in fact, shared country secrets with Soussoudis. They were not sure what and how much information was shared between Scranage and Soussoudis, but the CIA made claims that Scranage had turned over files and important documents on almost all of the CIA employees. The affair that went on between May 7, 1983, and October 1984 spelled disaster for the CIA.

Scranage was working as an Operations Support Assistant in Ghana. She shared secretive and confidential information with her boyfriend Michael Soussoudis. Soussoudis wasn't an ordinary Ghanaian citizen. He was much more than that. He was an intelligence officer with a permanent U.S. citizenship. He was given the job of laying down a honey trap by the Ghanaian intelligence to get Scranage out in the open and to get her talking about national security matters, and she fell right into this trap. According to CIA reports, Scranage gave information on eight Ghanaian citizens who had been carrying out espionage operations for the CIA. Scranage also unveiled the plans of a certain group of Ghanaian anarchists who were planning to take down the government. When Kojo Tsikata, the intelligence chief, got wind of these plans, he took immediate action. All of the spies that were working for the CIA were apprehended and charged with treason.

Scranage was tried on grounds of espionage and violating the Intelligence Identities Protection Act. She confessed to her crimes and was sentenced to five years in a federal prison. The sentence was later shortened to two years and then to a mere eight months.

Larry Wu-Tai Chin

The birthplace of Wu-Tai Chin was Beijing. He worked as a translator for the U.S. Government and also provided his services as a translator in World War II. He served as a translator for many U.S. departments which included the U.S. consulate in Shanghai, the State Department and the CIA's Foreign Broadcast Information Service.

He carried out espionage missions with great efficiency for China for thirty years. He informed the Chinese government of Richard Nixon's diplomatic motives and intentions behind his visit, and China was able to devise a strategy to hold successful talks with Nixon based on this information. The secretive and classified information provided by Larry was then passed on to the Vietnamese agencies by Chinese officials.

Chin was able to secure many acres of real estate, including 29 rental properties. He was paid handsomely for his services as a spy by the Chinese government. He had to find a way to hide his espionage payments from the U.S. Government. He developed a compulsive gambling habit for this very purpose.

He was found guilty and sent to a federal prison where he committed suicide by suffocating himself with a plastic bag.

Randy Miles Jeffries

Randy Miles Jeffries worked under the payroll of the FBI as a clerk from 1978 to 1980. He was caught in 1983 by the police and sentenced to one year in prison for heroin possession. The judge decreed that he had to attend rehab as well to recover from his heroin addiction. A stenography and reporting firm by the name of Acme Reporting Company contracted with the FBI, and Randy was chosen to handle classified documents and to dispose of them in a garbage container. Jeffries, abetted by a colleague, tried to sell secret information to the Soviet Military Office in 1985. The Soviet Military Office promised to pay him 60 dollars for these documents, and Jeffries went through with the trade. He was exposed by an undercover FBI agent who was working for the Soviet regime.

Reports coming out of concerned agencies showed that the security systems in Acme Reporting Company were outmoded and flawed. There was no check and balance of employees. Personnel and manpower was assigned without any background checks, and the employees were allowed to take classified documents to their homes for handling and analyzing purposes.

Jeffries was sentenced to nine years in federal prison.

Edward Lee Howard

Edward Lee Howard was another case of an official gone bad. Edward Lee Howard had quite a promising career before he was kicked out of the CIA, which eventually forced his hand to plot against them. In his early years, he was a Boy Scout, an altar boy and a generous and kind-hearted Peace Corps Volunteer doing his duties in the drug capital of the world, Colombia. Edward worked on many assignments pertaining to international development work with the United States Agency for International Development (USAID). Shortly after that, the CIA called him up and recruited him because they thought he might be a valuable asset for the intelligence organization.

The CIA found out on May 1983 that Edward Lee Howard had a dark past. They made him take a polygraph test which he failed. The CIA had no choice but to relieve him of his duties. Howard was angry and disappointed with the way the CIA treated him. He made phone calls from an unsecure line to the U.S. embassy in Moscow while he was drunk and revealed that his former supervisor was, in fact, a CIA employee. He knew that these calls were tapped by the Soviet agencies.

In 1984, Howard was accused of giving confidential information to KGB operatives in Austria. He made contact with them and gave them important files and documents and told them about his recollections in the CIA. He found refuge in the New Mexico desert after he was ratted out by Vitaly Yurchenko. He was on the CIA radar and had to find a safe haven, and this was the perfect place for him. The CIA was tricked by Howard's wife who drove to the desert with a decoy passenger in the driving seat and one of Howard's voice recordings. The Russians were generous enough to grant Howard asylum after he slipped through the clutches of the CIA.

This crackdown on espionage operations was due to President Ronald Reagan's continued efforts. He provisioned resources and personnel to different intelligence agencies and equipped them with the tools and the power to tighten the noose on these masters of disguise. However, this still does not explain the increasing influx of defectors and the highly commendable work of the family members to identify these spies and inform on them to the police. So, it was the combined meticulous work of the people and the government that led to the apprehension of people who were a serious threat to national security.

One thing that is noteworthy here is that the number of spies at the end of the Cold War was a lot more than it was before it started. This statistic tells us that a lot more spies were planted into different governments, which meant that there was a greater possibility of spies being caught as well. A large number of spies were also disillusioned by their corresponding intelligence agencies tossing them into a sea of landmines because they were considered a liability and a ticking time bomb just waiting to explode.

The secrets were floating freely in the air after the Cold War, and many spies had easy access to these secrets. Many spies considered this as a door of opportunity and took their chance. Most of the spies in the '80s traded important information for money to make sure that their future was filled with wealth and riches. You can think of the spies in the '80s as drug dealers. The only difference was that the drug that they were selling was a blunt of secrets, and there were a lot of junkies and addicts in different intelligence agencies that were willing to pay top dollar for a small dose of these secrets. This led to a marked increase in cloak-and-dagger operations in the upcoming years.

This crazy spy legacy was inherited by the spies of contemporary times. Espionage operations only slightly declined during the 1990s. After the harrowing 9/11 incident, many intelligence agencies incorporated a fresh influx of talented spies which further increased the number of covert operations pertinent to espionage. Espionage is the past, the present and the future, and it is quite disturbing to know that there is no indication of it disappearing in the future. As long as greed and disloyalty run in human veins, betrayal and treason will foreshadow honesty and patriotism.

3. Violent Crime/Major Thefts/Bank Robberies

3.1 Brinks Robbery

Introduction

On January 17, 1950, when the clock was about to strike 7:30 p.m., the "crime of the century" was committed by 11 gang members. This "perfect crime" that completely baffled the whole of America was executed with such precision and was so meticulous in its planning that it took the FBI six long years to catch and arrest the perpetrators.

The Brink's Building, which was the victim of the robbery, is located in the North End of Boston at 165 Prince Street. The robbery was carried out by 11 gang members, namely: Joseph "Big Joe" McGinnis, Joseph "Specs" O'Keefe, Anthony Pino, Stanley "Gus" Gusciora, Vincent Costa, Michael Vincent "Vinnie Jean" Jacquouille, Thomas "Sandy" Francis Richardson, Adolf H. "Jazz" Maffei, Henry Conan, James "Guillemets" Faherty, and Joseph Banfield. The first four members of the gang were the main culprits behind the crime. It was a very well researched plan and took the members almost five years to formulate.

While the gang members were very careful not to leave any sort of clues at the crime scene, the FBI still managed to catch them somehow, albeit it took them six years. How did they get caught if none of the members made a single blunder or left any clues during the execution of the crime? Well, the FBI can thank Joseph O'Keefe, or "Specs", for that. O'Keefe was sent to prison in 1950, not for the Brink's Robbery, but for another minor burglary, and while being held for interrogation, he decided to rat out on his fellow gang members.

$1,000,000 in Cash Seized By 7 Masked Men in Boston

By JOHN H. FENTON

Special to The New York Times

BOSTON, Jan. 17—One of the nation's biggest cash robberies was staged tonight by seven masked men who took "more than $1,000,000" from the vault room of an armored trucking service.

Police Superintendent Edward W. Fallon, who made the estimate, said the men left "almost as much more, because they couldn't carry it away."

Wearing orange and black Halloween masks, the seven armed bandits, working with a precision that indicated long planning, overpowered five employes of Brink's, Inc., on the Boston waterfront, bound and gagged them and fled

DRISCOLL ATTACKS FEDERAL SPENDING

Starting Second Term, Jersey Governor Sees Inflationary

Credit: Timothy Hughes Rare Newspapers

The Mastermind behind the Robbery

The Brink's Company is responsible for dealing with millions of dollars every day. Tony "Fats" Pino, the mastermind behind the crime, was well aware of this fact. Pino was a small-time criminal, robbing stores, shoplifting, and carrying out small heists. He had been to prison over 20 times. But no matter how many times he was thrown into jail for his petty crimes, he always came out with the same agenda: to rob stores and get money. It did not take him very long to figure out that he was too smart to be robbing small stores and it was time he needed to do something that would leave the authorities banging their heads against the wall. So, when Pino got out of prison in 1944, it took him only a year to start sketching some very well thought out ideas for the Great Brink's Robbery.

Why did Tony choose to rob the Brink's Building and not any other big company? He noticed that the staff at Brink's Company was incredibly lean when it came to dealing with a big amount of money. He observed the company from afar and he realized that it was possible to rob the company and easily get away with it. Pino carefully developed the plan for five years. For five years, he inspected the structure of the building and internal workings of the company, the behavior of the staff. He would go inside the building while wearing disguises to understand the details of the building and learn on what days the company held the highest amount of money inside the building.

Tony soon started to realize that while the robbery was possible, he needed partners. He needed people who would help him carry out the heist, and he knew that he needed a lot of people; for a crime of this magnitude, two or three partners were not going to help at all. So, he started recruiting people, people like himself -- small-time criminals, mostly people he knew from his time in jail. Some of the first members he took in with him were Joseph "Specs" O'Keefe, Joseph "Big Joe" McGinnis, and Stanley "Gus" Gusciora. It didn't take very long for him to find the rest of the members of the gang. Pino was very well acquainted with people who worked in this line of business, and his gang soon had all the eleven members it needed to carry out the heist.

The Gang and Preparation for the Heist

For five years, the gang regularly snuck into the building when they knew the staff had emptied it and there was no one in it. Pino had carefully learned the schedule of the entire staff and knew when everyone went in and out of the building. The whole gang would sneak into the building for rehearsals on a regular basis. Sometimes, they inspected the building from nearby rooms which were occupied by the gang. Pino's brother-in-law, Vincent Costa, owned a room in a building that was situated right across Prince Street (where the Brink's Building was located) from where he would regularly observe the depot where the money was stored.

The gang stole keys from Brink's North Terminal Garage to vehicles that belonged to the Company and used them to regularly rob the vehicles and steal a huge amount of cash. It wasn't only the Company Pino's gang stole from; they stole from the safes of Brink's customers, too. The gang noticed when the customers would have the highest amount of money available in their safes and then steal from them whenever they would get a chance. According to one report, the gang managed to make off with over four thousand dollars, stolen from both the Company and its customers, all before they even committed the "crime of the century".

Brink's security wasn't very advanced and, as mentioned before, the staff was very lean when it came to handling large amounts of money. There was only one alarm that stood in the gang's way, and it was installed on the company vault, but even this was not going to be a problem for the gang for very long. They continuously broke into the building to get as much information about the workings of the alarms as they could. They learned everything there was to learn about the security of the Building, and it didn't take the gang too long to understand that Brink's was too lenient with their security. You would think that after doing so much research on the company's security system, the gang would've figured out a way to get rid of the alarm on the vault, but they didn't. They did, however, find a way to get past it. They would simply change the status of their robbery from mere burglary to armed robbery and they would go in when the vault was open.

The gang exchanged a lot of different ideas before finally settling on this one. The initial plan was to sneak in the building at night and stay inside until morning when the employees showed up and then take them as hostage. But O'Keefe, who was probably the most intelligent person in the gang, knew that this was not how things were going to work. He developed the idea that the gang would get rid of the lock cylinders by making duplicate keys for the locks. He thought if they did this, then they would easily be able to carry out the heist without anyone taking notice of what had been done. The gang decided that they would send seven of its members inside the building with the keys and deploy the drivers outside the building so the men inside could make their getaway as fast as possible. They stole the uniforms of Brink's so as not to encounter any problem while breaking into the building. The gang was now all ready to execute the crime of the century.

The Heist

At 6:55 p.m. on January 17, 1950, O'Keefe and six other men entered the Brink's Building. They wore the uniforms of Brink's employees and one other strange object: Halloween masks. To make sure that their shoes wouldn't produce any loud or unnecessary sound, they wore rubber-soled shoes. Every action of the members served as a testament to the intellect and genius of the gang members. They carefully snuck up on the Brink's employees, silently entering the locked doors with the duplicate keys, forced them to lie down on the floor and tied them up. As soon as they tied them up and gagged them, they started moving all the money to a truck they had parked outside the building. They moved everything they could find to the truck, everything but one payroll box that belonged to the General Electric (GE) Company.

Not a single clue was left at the scene of the robbery; the only thing they left was the rope they used to tie up the employees and the tape they used to gag them. They left the

Top Cases of The FBI – Volume 2

building at 7:30 p.m. and transported all the money to a safe house where they had agreed to meet up so they could distribute it. The whole thing happened so fast that the employees didn't even get the time to make sense of their situation.

During the robbery, a garage attendant, unaware of what was going on inside the building, attempted to enter the vault area. The robbers learned about this from one of the employees, after they removed the gag from their mouth. Two members of the gang decided that if the attendant entered the vault, they would jump him and tie him down, too, with the rest of the employees. They positioned themselves at the door and got ready to grab him, but the garage attendant decided not to enter the vault and went back. The gang resumed putting the money in their bags. The total amount of money that they managed to steal was more than $2 million.

The crime was committed with utmost precision and caution. It could easily be considered the epitome of how the perfect crime should be committed. No evidence was left at the scene and the members made absolutely no blunders -- except one. O'Keefe had to go to prison for a minor burglary he had committed. For this reason, he had to put his share of the money somewhere safe. He

88

decided to leave it with one of the members of the gang. This was going to prove to be the downfall of the whole gang after six years.

The Investigation

As soon as the word got out that $2 million dollars had been stolen from the Brink's Building, the Boston Police were stunned. Who had stolen the money and how had they managed to steal so much of it without leaving a single clue? Over 100 officers were called by Edward Fallon, the Superintendent of Boston Police, and he told them about what had happened. No sooner had they been briefed about the robbery than the hoodlums of Boston started being interrogated. Employees of Brink's were questioned, and even the people who had called before the robbery were interrogated, yet the police found no answers.

Soon enough, however, the police found some things which they thought might give them some clues as to the identities of the robbers. During the heist, four revolvers were stolen, one of them was found by a police officer at Mystic River in Somerville. After the heist, the gang had disposed of the getaway truck by cutting it into pieces and throwing them away at a junk yard in Stoughton,

Massachusetts. It was found that the pieces of the truck had been smashed with a hammer. Some of the pieces were later found by Bureau agents. These clues, however, did not help them in finding the robbers. Despite all the leads they had, neither the police nor the FBI could find the gang. Brink's had offered a reward of $100,000 to anyone who could provide any sort of information regarding the crime to the police. This led to many Americans coming up with their own theories, and many of them started sending their theories to the FBI in the hope that they would help them catch members of the gang.

None of the theories, however, proved to be helpful, and they only served to confuse the police and the FBI more than they already were. Someone suggested that a man seen in Bayonne, New Jersey, could have been involved in the robbery. The man was said to have been spending more money than he had been normally known to spend. He was buying new cars, spending his money in clubs, etc. The FBI decided to look into the matter but found the person innocent. The FBI also investigated members that belonged to the "Purple Gang", a group that had been active in the 1930s, and another gang which used to smuggle whiskey during the Prohibition era, but still found no answers.

Two years after the robbery, on January 17, a phone call was made at the FBI's Boston Office by an anonymous person who sent a letter in which names of the people who had carried out the heist were listed. Nine hoodlums were named in the letter; eight of them were ruled out as being the perpetrators of the crime, but the ninth person turned out to be a member of the gang and he was later (much later) arrested. Many hoodlums who were serving time in prison saw this crime as an opportunity to get out of the place by claiming to have information while being interrogated but saying that they would only reveal the information they had if they were released.

The authorities were so distraught by this incident that the FBI decided to investigate anyone who was in possession of more money than they were usually known to have, especially after the crime was committed. They even investigated race tracks and gamblers. The FBI's actions left many gamblers feeling upset, and some of them demanded that the criminals responsible for carrying out the heist should be arrested as soon as possible. Some, however, were so disappointed by this that they decided to shut down their casinos.

After removing the names of thousands of suspects from the list of people who could've committed the crime, the FBI finally started to narrow down the list. Pino had been a suspect for a very long time; he was famous for committing heists. But when he was interrogated, he said he had been at a liquor store at 7:00 p.m. along with McGinnis. He said he had been talking to a Boston police officer, and the officer later confirmed that he did, in fact, meet Pino. But the liquor store was very close to the Brink's Building, so the FBI soon started to suspect that he might have left for the liquor store with McGinnis after carrying out the heist at 7:30 p.m.

The FBI knew that a crime this big could not have been committed by two people alone. They knew McGinnis and Pino were big players in the crime scene, and they knew they'd had more partners to help them with the robbery. O'Keefe and Gusciora were suspected to be Pino and McGinnis's accomplices. O'Keefe had been involved with both Gusciora and Pino in other crimes in the past. When interrogated, Gusciora and O'Keefe both claimed that they had been drinking at a bar at the time of the robbery.

The Gang Finally Breaks the Silence

Rumors started spreading around that many criminals were being forced to pay for

O'Keefe and Gusciora's release, both of whom had been sentenced to serve time in prison for other crimes. The names of Pino and McGinnis were frequently mentioned. Many of the criminals involved in the heist were interrogated, including Pino's brother-in-law, Vincent James Costa. The FBI realized something strange during the interrogation. All of the suspects said they had been doing something at 7 p.m. The FBI now almost knew that they had identified the perpetrators, but they still lacked evidence.

When O'Keefe got out of prison in 1954, he learned that the other members of the gang had spent most of his money and he felt cheated. The animosity between O'Keefe and other members increased to such a level that it resulted in O'Keefe kidnapping Vincent Costa and demanding ransom of over a thousand dollars. Some part of the ransom was paid and O'Keefe released Costa. The FBI investigated Costa, Pino, and O'Keefe regarding the incident, but all of them denied it ever having happened.

Attempts were made by the gang to assassinate O'Keefe because they felt he was going to betray them. They hired a hitman and made attempts on O'Keefe's life three times. The hitman, named Elmer "Trigger" Burke, was caught by the Boston police and he revealed that he had been hired by someone to kill

O'Keefe. O'Keefe was arrested on August 1, 1954, and he was to spend the next 27 months in jail.

O'Keefe had reached a point where the FBI figured if they pushed him enough, he would confess or rat on his fellow gang members. O'Keefe frequently wrote letters to the members saying he wanted his money, most of which had been spent by the members, back. O'Keefe realized that he was in a very difficult situation; he could either choose to turn against his comrades and ask the FBI for protection or he could rot in prison while the members of the gang enjoyed their lives and spent all of his money. He also knew that as soon as he got out, the gang would try to have him assassinated again.

On January 6, 1956, O'Keefe, feeling betrayed by his former gang members, finally decided to tell the FBI everything. The FBI confirmed his story, most of which they had already known, thanks to the investigation they carried out for six long years. O'Keefe provided the details of the story the FBI didn't and couldn't figure out.

Arrests

Six members of the gang were arrested – Baker, Costa, Geagan, Maffie, McGinnis, and

Pino. O'Keefe and Gusciora were already in prison. One member was dead, and the remaining two had escaped and were added to the FBI's list of "Ten Most Wanted Fugitives". However, they were soon arrested, too. Much of the cash that was stolen, however, was never retrieved. O'Keefe did not have any knowledge regarding the whereabouts of the stolen money, and the other gang members refused to say anything. Some part of the money was found at a hotel in Baltimore by the FBI.

Eight members of the gang were proven guilty, thanks to O'Keefe, who told the court the details of the crime and the roles of all of the members. All eight of them were thrown into prison. According to O'Keefe, before the crime was committed, all the members of the gang had made an agreement to "take care of" anyone who "muffed". O'Keefe felt that the whole gang had "muffed" and he took care of them by giving all the information to the FBI.

3.2 Black Dahlia

Introduction

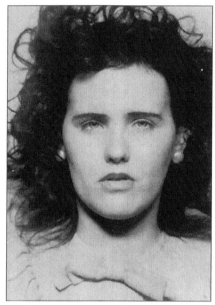

Mug shots and fingerprint of Elizabeth Short
Credit: of the FBI

On January 15, 1947, the body of a 22-year-old woman was discovered in Los Angeles. This woman was identified by the FBI as Elizabeth Short, nicknamed Black Dahlia. Her dead body was found near the sidewalk, cut in half. To this day, the killer of Elizabeth Short still remains unknown, and the crime, because of its mysterious aura, continues to fascinate people.

Early Life

Elizabeth Short was born to Cleo and Phoebe May Short in Boston, Massachusetts. Her father was known to build miniature golf courses for a living, but when the stock market crashed in 1929 and America entered the Great Depression era, Cleo Short had to find another job. The economic crisis that lasted from 1929 to 1939 took a heavy toll on Elizabeth's father, and he ended up losing almost all of his money. Driven by despair and guilt, he tried to run away from his family and his responsibilities.

He parked his car near a bridge so people would think that he had committed suicide by jumping into the river. After his disappearance, Elizabeth's mother, Phoebe, took her daughter and moved with her into an apartment in a suburb of Boston. She first got a job as a bookkeeper to support her daughter, but she continued to change jobs, sometimes working two jobs at once.

They were also supported by their relatives who helped them with their finances and took care of Elizabeth. Elizabeth and her mother did not learn about her husband's disappearance until he wrote them a letter in which he explained that he was living in California now but wanted to come see her and Elizabeth. Phoebe, angry with her husband, told him that she did not want to see him again and refused to let him come back.

Elizabeth was very popular among her friends. Her friends called her "Betty", "Bette", or "Beth". From a young age, Elizabeth was intrigued by the world of cinema and movies. Oftentimes, she would go to the theater whenever the world became too much for her to handle. She considered it an escape from her mundane life. Her friends used to say that she was mature for her age and described her as looking older than she was. She suffered from asthma and always had lung problems, and her mother recommended her to spend the winter of 1940 in Miami, Florida.

Despite her struggle with asthma and bronchitis, she was still a very active person.

From 1940 to 1943, she stayed in Miami, Florida, during the winter and stayed with her mother in Medford for the rest of the year. Despite her mother's refusal to see Elizabeth's father, Elizabeth kept in touch with him and they wrote letters to each other back and forth. Cleo soon asked her if she could come and visit him in California. He was willing to let her stay with him in his apartment. Elizabeth had always wanted to be a movie star, and she saw this as an opportunity to accomplish her dreams. She knew that if she ever went to California, she would not come back until she had fulfilled her dreams and become a movie star. She packed up her bags and soon moved in with her father in California.

Things, however, soon became unstable between Elizabeth and her father. Her father was a strict man and could not tolerate laziness and bad housekeeping, traits which were openly exhibited by Elizabeth. Elizabeth and Cleo Short would have arguments on a daily basis, and the relationship between them got worse every day. She was known to be very outgoing and was always going out on a date. Every week, she would have a new boyfriend with whom she would be going out on a date.

Her father could not handle all of her bad habits and, in 1943, he decided to kick her out of the house. Elizabeth was now all alone and jobless.

Trouble with the Law

She soon recovered from her torpor and got a job as a cashier at the Post Exchange at Camp Cooke. She participated in a beauty contest that took place at the Camp, and she was rewarded with the title of "Camp Cutie of

Camp Cooke". At this period of her life, Elizabeth was suffering from depression, and she wanted her life to become stable, showing a desire for a permanent relationship instead of going out on a date with a different person every night. She did not like the work at Camp Cooke, and when she got the chance, she quit and moved in with a girlfriend in Santa Barbara.

This was the only time when she had had a problem with the law. On September 23, 1943, she went out with her friends to a restaurant. The group started shouting and disturbing other people who were seated at the restaurant, and the owner, who had grown tired of their behavior by now, called the police. Elizabeth was taken to the prison for underage drinking and a mugshot was taken of her, but she was never arrested. The police officer who had brought her in felt bad for her and he sent her back to Massachusetts, but Elizabeth, driven by her obsession with movies, soon moved back to California.

Elizabeth had been looking to settle down for a while now, and while she was in Los Angeles, she met a pilot named Gordon Fickling. Fickling and Elizabeth soon fell in love and wanted to marry each other. They made plans, but all of them went to waste when Fickling was deployed to Europe and became separated from Elizabeth.

Elizabeth was now alone, but she did not allow her mind to drift into a constant state of sadness. She started working as a model and managed to make some money for herself, but soon left the job because she did not feel satisfied with it. She moved back to Medford and lived with her mother there for a while, but she knew in her heart that this was not what she wanted to do. Following her instincts, she moved back to live in Miami with her relatives.

She had become tired of being alone all the time and she still wanted to get married. She dated some servicemen for a time and soon met a man named Matthew Michael Gordon, Jr. Matt Gordon was a U.S. Army Air Force officer who worked in the 2nd Air Commando Group. Matt was deployed to the China-Burma-India (CBI) Theater during World War II.

She told her friends that Matt had written to her while he was in India, asking for her hand in marriage. Matt's plane had crashed when he had written the supposed letter and he was being treated for his injuries. Things were finally looking good for Elizabeth and Matt, and they made plans to get married as soon as Matt returned. Matt, however, died when his plane crashed again on August 10, 1945, a week before the Japanese surrendered and the war ended. Elizabeth was shocked when she found out Matt had died. She started telling her friends that she had married Matt before he left and they had a baby who died in childbirth.

When Elizabeth finally recovered from her depression, she tried to get in touch with her old friends who worked in Hollywood. One of the people she reconnected with was her ex-boyfriend, Gordon Fickling. She started writing to Fickling, thinking it would help her forget about Matt Gordon, and after some time, decided to meet him in Chicago. She fell in love with him again and spent some time with him in Long Beach. But she was still obsessed with becoming a movie star and she was not ready to give up on her dreams, and so she moved back to California again. Before she left for San Diego on December 8, 1946, Mark Hansen, a friend of Elizabeth's, reported that she looked very distressed and there was clearly something that was bothering her. When he was questioned by Frank Jemison on December 16, 1949, Mark Hansen said that he saw her crying in her apartment and she kept repeating that she "had to get out of there". He reported that she looked very scared.

She still went to San Diego and met a woman there named Dorothy French. Dorothy worked as a counter girl at the Aztec Theater, and she struck up a conversation with Elizabeth after she found her sleeping in the theater after an evening show. Elizabeth told Dorothy why she ran away from Hollywood, saying it was not easy to work as an actress because of the actors' strikes. Elizabeth did not have any place where she could sleep, so Dorothy invited her to stay at her mother's place for some days. Elizabeth ended up staying there for almost a month.

Last Days

Elizabeth did not curtail her bad habits, and she continued dating different men on a regular basis while she was staying at Dorothy French's mother's house. She did not even take up any work at the house. She found herself dating a man named Robert "Red" Manley, a married salesman whose wife was pregnant.

When Manley was questioned after Elizabeth's murder, he said that he only found her attractive and never slept with her. Elizabeth once asked him to take her back to Hollywood. Manley picked her up on January 8, 1947, and took her to a hotel. He paid for all the expenses and even took her to a party that night. Manley spent the night at the hotel room with Elizabeth, but he slept on the bed while she slept in a chair.

Manley was supposed to go somewhere in the morning, but he came back for Elizabeth in the afternoon. Elizabeth told Manley that she wanted to go back to Massachusetts but wanted to see her sister, who was staying at Biltmore Hotel in Hollywood, before leaving. She asked Manley to take her to the hotel and he agreed, but he left after dropping her off at the hotel. This was going to be the last time Manley saw Elizabeth Short. Elizabeth went missing for six days and her body, which was cut into two, was discovered on January 15, 1947.

On that day, a woman named Betty Bersinger went out with her three-year-old daughter. She was on her way to the shoe repair shop, completely unaware of what she was going to find on that eerie morning. Because of the war, construction of buildings had slowed down and, as a result, there had been many vacant lots in the city. Betty was walking with her daughter near the sidewalk when her eyes darted towards a white object in the bushes. When she first saw it, she thought it was a mannequin and it had been slashed in half. She became curious and decided to get a closer look and was horrified and shocked at what she found. She screamed and quickly hid her daughter from the gruesome sight. She immediately went to the nearest house and called the police.

Warning: Crime Scene Photos on the next two pages.

Crime Scene Photos

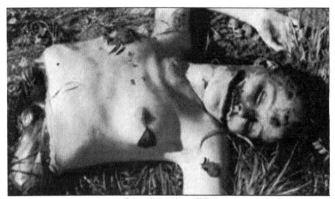

Credit: the FBI

Investigation

Two police officers arrived at the crime scene, and when they confirmed the account of Betty Bersinger, they called for backup. The police realized that someone had staged the body in a way so as to make it look like it was posing. Elizabeth Short's corpse was lying on the ground with her face towards the sky, her legs left wide open, and her arms were raised higher than her shoulders. The killer had slashed her mouth from her lips to both of her ears, a cut that is more popularly known as a Glasgow Smile. Because of the rope marks on her body, the police believed that she had been tortured before she was killed. Her body had been cut in two pieces and there was no blood around the crime scene which suggested that this was not the place where the killer had murdered her, but a dumping area.

Due to the grotesque nature of the crime, two senior detectives were assigned to the case: Detective Sergeant Harry Hansen and Detective Finnis Brown. Before they could reach the crime scene, a crowd had gathered around it. The detectives were angry when they found out that there were civilians gathered around the dead body. Feeling afraid that the public would contaminate the evidence, he had everyone removed.

The body was transferred to the Los Angeles County Morgue where it was to be examined and identified. The police took the body's fingerprints and sent them to the FBI so that they could find out who the dead person was. Because of the bad weather, sending information to the FBI had proved to be a little troublesome, and it was thought that it would take over a week before they could get the prints to the FBI for identification. But thanks to Warden Woolard, editor of The Herald Express, the police were able to speed up the process.

According to Woolard, The Herald Express was in possession of a machine called "Soundphoto". With this machine, Woolard could send the fingerprints to the FBI very quickly. The FBI, at first, had difficulty in identifying the fingerprints because they could not be read, but then a photographer who worked at Herald Express told the police that they should send negative prints of the fingerprints to the FBI. He also enlarged the size of the prints which made it easier for the FBI to read them. The FBI soon had all the information they needed about the dead body. The victim was Elizabeth Short, 22, who worked at Camp Cooke and was last known to live in Santa Barbara.

When the body was examined in the

coroner's office, it was revealed that her corpse had been cleaned before being thrown away. This made it harder to tell what the killer had done to the body. There were, however, a lot of cuts on the body near the pubic area, and it was believed that the killer had cut the body postmortem. The FBI determined that Elizabeth had died of "hemorrhage and shock" because of "concussion of the brain and lacerations of the face."

When Elizabeth's mother, Phoebe, was told that her daughter had been murdered, she was aghast and found herself unwilling to believe that her daughter was dead. Wayne Sutton, a re-write man for the Herald Express, was the one who broke the news to Phoebe. However, before telling her the truth, he told her lies so that he could glean information about her daughter. He knew that if he told her the truth before getting some background, she would be unwilling to cooperate and would not give as much information. So, he told her that Elizabeth had won in a beauty contest and started asking questions about her daughter. As soon as he had all the data he needed, Sutton told Phoebe the truth.

The LAPD instructed the local Medford cops to go to Phoebe's house and confirm the story for her because she refused to believe Sutton.

Pretty soon, The Herald Express had started receiving anonymous calls and letters which gave clues and information regarding the murder. It was found that Elizabeth used to keep photographs of her friends and herself in a trunk, but the trunk had not been found after being shipped to Los Angeles from Chicago. The Herald Express found the trunk at the Greyhound Express station in Los Angeles and, through the pictures, they tried to understand who Elizabeth Short was. The Herald put up a picture of Elizabeth on the front page of the newspaper on January 17, 1947, two days after the body had been found. They gave her the nickname "The Black Dahlia", owing to the fact that Elizabeth was mostly seen in black dresses and because of the movie called "Blue Dahlia" that had come out nine months before the murder. The murder was also referred to as the "Werewolf Murder".

Do You Know This Girl?

This is a photograph of an unidentified teen-aged girl found slain in a vacant lot on Norton avenue near Coliseum avenue. Picture was taken in death, but with marks of violence removed.

Credit: Front page of the Herald Express, January 17, 1947

The Killer

It was believed that whoever the killer was, they had killed because they held a grudge against Short. The killer threw away the body in a place where it could easily be discovered because they wanted it to be found. According to Dr. Paul De River, the murderer was a sadist who wanted to have total control over Elizabeth Short. Dr. De River also suggested that the killer might have been a necrophiliac, (however because the body was cleaned, there was no evidence of anyone having sex with the corpse). According to him, the killer wanted to show that he or she was dominant and the master, and Elizabeth was the slave.

The FBI's office was flooded with letters from people who claimed to be the killer. One anonymous caller told The Examiner that, to prove he was the person who had killed Elizabeth Short, he was going to send them a package that included Elizabeth's birth certificate, photographs, etc. And he did send it. He also included an address book that had the name "Mark Hansen" written on it. Because of this, Mark Hansen became one of the prime suspects in the case.

Some other belongings of Elizabeth were discovered by Robert "Red" Manley in a trash can on the same day. This suggested that the killer lived in the vicinity of the vacant lot where Elizabeth's dead body was found.

Many people anonymously called the LAPD and sent letters, giving tips and information; most of them turned out to be nothing but hoaxes. Some of these letters, however, were suspected to have been written by the killer himself, but it was almost impossible to determine what was written in them, because most of the things written in them were incoherent and undecipherable. The LAPD believed that the killer was trying to mock the detectives with these letters. All the things that were sent to the LAPD did not have any fingerprints on them, so it was impossible to determine the sender from these, too.

Some people who were thought to have killed Elizabeth were: Mark Hansen, Sergeant "Chuck", Doctor George Hodel, Doctor Patrick S. O'Reilly, Doctor Paul DeGaston, Glenn Wolf, Marvin Margolis, etc. etc. No evidence could be gathered against any of them, though, and the case remains unsolved even today.

4. Civil Rights

4.1 Missississippi Burning: *The violent Murders of Chaney, Goodman and Schwerner and the events that ensued.*

Freedom Summer, a civil rights movement, was put into existence to clinch the well-deserved right to vote for the disenfranchised potential black voters of the southern United States. This campaign amassed thousands of supporters in the form of students and activists who fearlessly campaigned for their political rights and became members of Congress of Racial Equality (CORE).

They rallied towards the southern states to encourage people to vote. However, this movement faced a brutal tragedy. Three civil rights workers were mercilessly killed by the terrorist organization, the Ku Klux Klan, which has a history of perpetrating violent crimes and disseminating hate in America.

Michael Schwerner and James Chaney

Michael Schwerner and James Chaney were still in their early twenties when they decided to fight for the rights of the black community of Neshoba County, Mississippi. Their main goal was to open freedom schools and to promote their campaign. They encouraged black people to take part in the coming elections and exercise their right to vote. White-owned businesses were facing difficult times because the black people of Mississippi refused to work for them due to the protests lodged by the freedom workers.

This incited the members of the Ku Klux Klan, and they began to devise a strategy to cleanse the area of some of the more well-known activists of the Freedom Summer movement. Michael Schwerner, dubbed as "Jew boy" by the anti-Semitic and racist Ku Klux Klan, was the first activist who caught the attention of the organization, after successfully organizing the Meridian boycott. The Ku Klux Klan felt threatened by the indomitable spirit of the civil rights activists who were ready to do everything in their power to ensure the voting rights of the black people of America.

Plan 4: Secret Operation devised to Kill Schwerner, Chaney and Goodman

The Ku Klux Klan was highly involved in the matters and activities of Mississippi during the 1960s. The Ku Klux Klan had big names in its ranks. It had people who held powerful positions in law enforcement, business, etc., and other spheres.

The White Knights were led by their Imperial Wizard Sam Bowers in those days. He despised Michael Schwerner and rebuked the work he was doing. Plan 4 was the name of the secret operation that was put into place to get rid of Schwerner. In May 1965, Bowers informed his members, who followed him blindly to the ends of hell, that Plan 4 was now ready to put into play. Schwerner had a meeting to attend in Mount Zion Church on June 16 and the Klan was well aware of that.

The Church held paramount importance for the civil rights activists as it was the assigned location for the development of many freedom schools in the future in Mississippi. The Klan, however, received wrong intel. When the Klan members, armed with heavy-duty machine guns, arrived there, there was no sign of Michael Schwerner, and this infuriated them. All this anger and rage led them to pummel and batter the church members, extracting information out of them regarding Schwerner and his colleagues. The whole church was burnt to the ground. Devastated by the news of the vicious and savage attack on the Church, Schwerner and Cheney decided to head back to Mount Zion to inquire about the incident.

Burning of the Church

Schwerner knew that there were occupational hazards in his line of work. So, he was extra cautious while approaching the whole matter as he knew that Mississippi was already a danger zone for civil rights activists. The group stayed in Meridian for a night, packed their bags in the morning and travelled to the burnt church in Mount Zion in the morning. They met with some of the members of the church who were beaten to a pulp by the Ku Klux Klan members.

The members of the church and other visitants told them that the real motive of the KKK attack was to find Schwerner and Chaney. They warned them about some white men who were looking for them, for all the wrong reasons.

They headed back to Meridian in an exposed and prominent blue CORE-owned Ford station wagon at noon. They told their associates that if they weren't back by 4:30 p.m., they should presume that they are in some sort of danger. They were spotted by a Klan member, Deputy Sheriff Cecil Price, who took immediate action against them. He not only impeded their progress back to Meridian but also placed them in police custody on grounds of allegedly setting the Mount Zion church on fire.

They were released shortly after on bail and chased out of town by Deputy Price in a white Chevrolet sedan. The three workers were out of the city after some time. They were en route south on Highway 19. They made a stop at the Pilgrims Store and had intentions of using the telephone to let their colleagues know their whereabouts, but they didn't go through with it because of the presence of a highway patrol car keeping a close eye on them. Consequently, they continued their journey towards Meridian.

A lynch mob followed the vehicle of Chaney and company. They were arguing with each other about who would do the deed. Finally, they were given orders by Barnett and Posy, who were designated police officials in Philadelphia. They told them to pursue the civil rights activists. The lynch mob travelled in two separate cars. One of the cars had some mechanical issues and was sidelined.

Price eventually caught up to the vehicle of the civil rights workers on Highway 492. He halted their progress and coerced them to turn around and go back to Philly. They all gathered on the intersection of County Road 515 where the lynch mob carried out the heinous act of killing Chaney and his associates. Chaney was beaten to a pulp before being shot.

After murdering the activists in cold blood, they carried their dead bodies to the Jolly Farm along Highway 21. There was a construction site near the Old Jolly Farm. An earthen dam was under construction for a farm pond. Herman Tucker, who had been given precise instructions, was waiting for the arrival of the Klan members. The lynch mob and Tucker had met beforehand and worked out all the details of their diabolical plan to get rid of the dead bodies of the three activists. They wanted to dispose of the bodies in a manner that no trace was left of them. Tucker mercilessly ran a bulldozer over the dead bodies to bury them under many layers of mud. The autopsy report later revealed red clay fragments in Andrew Goodman's lungs which pointed to the fact that he was still alive when he was buried adjacent to his colleagues.

Role of the FBI in the Mississippi Attacks

The police inquired about the civil rights workers after their sudden disappearance. CORE workers made calls to the county jail asking them about the whereabouts of their workers, but the police refused to give out any information and denied their involvement in their arrests. What happened after their arrest? No one knew for sure.

On June 23, the FBI got involved and sent a team of ten men to thoroughly investigate the sudden disappearance of Schwerner and Chaney. The KKK never anticipated the attention the disappearance of the civil rights workers would draw towards them. They were naïve enough to think that they could just dispose of the workers as trash and get away with it. However, J. Edgar Hoover was pressured by President Lyndon B. Johnson to solve this mystery and find the perpetrators responsible for the disappearance of two young valiant men.

J. Edgar Hoover didn't take the matter seriously at first because he was against civil rights movements because of their alleged ties with communist regimes. He initially sent a team of ten FBI agents to Meridian to get to the root cause of the disappearance of the civil rights activists and unveil the underlying lurid details of this case to the public. The search was accelerated when U.S. Attorney General Robert F. Kennedy sent federal agents in large numbers, 150 to be precise, to New Orleans. The charred car was reported to the FBI by two Native Americans who spotted it on the county road. Joseph Sullivan immediately arrived at the designated place and scrutinized the entire crime scene.

The first FBI office in Mississippi was opened, and the military Naval bus station sent sailors into Neshoba County to help search for the missing men. The case with the code name MIBURN was launched by the FBI, and FBI agents having an impeccable success rate were sent to solve this case. A flock of sailors were commanded by the Naval Air bus station in Meridian to look for the dead bodies in the nearby swamps of Bogue Chitto.

In the search for the missing civil rights students, the searchers inadvertently stumbled upon the dead bodies of two college students by the names of Henry Hezekiah Dee and Charles Eddie Moore in the nearby areas. They had been missing since May 1964. Further investigation led to the revelation that they were kidnapped, brutally murdered and disposed of by white supremacists. Fourteen-year-old Herbert Oarsby and five unfortunate black women fell victim to the malicious and sinister savages of the Ku Klux Klan and were also found buried, by federal searchers.

The media was all over the Mississippi tragedy, and major news networks were desperate to know about every little detail of the case. This involved the public as well. Some of the news outlets described the disappearances as a national priority. The FBI vowed to offer a staggering reward of $25,000 to anyone who had any concrete information regarding the case. They wanted help in leading the FBI to the miscreants who were the masterminds of this violence.

FBI Investigation

The FBI was finally able to make sense of the events that caused the disappearance of the civil rights activists in Mississippi during the summer of 1965. FBI had planted informants in the Ku Klux Klan who gave vital information to the FBI regarding the murders of Chaney and his co-workers.

When Schwerner was arrested by Sheriff Cecil Price, he made a formal request to make a telephone call to Neshoba County, but he was turned down. Price informed Klansmen and told him that Schwerner was in his custody. Edgar Ray Killen passed on the information to a Klan group by the name of "butt ripping" and a meeting between Klan members was set up at a drive-in in Meridian. Shortly after, it was decided in another meeting that some of the younger Klansmen would carry out the assassination of Chaney and his associates. The Klan members met at 8:15 p.m. and devised a strategy to carry out the entire plan with efficacy.

They reviewed every little detail and made plans to kill the activists accordingly. They purchased rubber gloves, complying with the instructions of Killen. Killen left town after arranging the whole thing. Schwerner and his colleagues were released by Price at 10 p.m. They were pursued in a patrol car on Highway 19. An enthralling cat-and-mouse chase between the CORE group and the lynch mob resulted in the surrender of the activists.

The three members of the Freedom Summer movement were thumped into Price's car, and Price and two cars of Klan members drove through Rock Cut Road to reach another uncharted destination. At this point, Chaney and company would have gotten an idea that they were destined for something miserable.

They were taken out of the car and one of the Klan members first put a bullet in Schwerner's head followed by Goodman and Chaney. The undercover FBI informant told the FBI in a clandestine meeting that Doyle Barnett was also in on this murderous plan and he also shot Chaney twice.

The bodies of the activists were taken to Olen Burrage's Old Jolly Farm. He was waiting for the Klansmen to reach his farm. The bodies were buried near a dam site on the farm. The FBI received a tip from one of its informants about the location of the dead bodies, and they rushed to the site to uncover it. They finally found the dead bodies of the civil rights activists after a tedious investigation.

The Informant

The Klan member, James Jordan, originally a spy for the FBI, had supplied them with enough information to initiate an all-out attack on the alleged murderers of the civil rights activists. He provided information that linked 19 members of the Ku Klux Klan to the murders of Schwerner, Chaney and Andrew Goodman. However, the crooked judicial system wasn't going to make it easy for justice to prevail.

Charges Dismissed

The judicial system initially failed to provide justice to the members of CORE; within a week, the charges on all 19 men were dropped. The judge dismissed the evidence provided by Jordan rendering it as mere hearsay.

Federal Judge William Harold Cox upheld the indictments on the 19 men arrested on charges of alleged murder. William Harold Cox was renowned for being a hardcore segregationist and stated that only Price and Rainey were to be held accountable for the murders as they acted under the color of state law. He dismissed the remaining 17 indictments.

Until March 1996, Cox's judgment wasn't challenged. But shortly after that, the Supreme Court took steps to reinstate 18 of the 19 original indictments. The jury was biased and took the side of the KKK on the matter. It was blatant that they had a secret agenda to make sure that the Klansmen didn't pay for their crimes. The jury was comprised of seven white men and five white women, including an ex-Ku Klux Klan member. Judge Cox even said that African Americans had a resemblance with chimpanzees, which further aggravated the prosecutors.

FBI informants working in the Ku Klux Klan gave testimony against the indicted Klan members. They described the details leading to the murder of the three men in front of the judge, and Jordan testified to the actual murder. His role in this should not be undervalued. He was adamant to incriminate the Ku Klux Klan members.

The defense consisted of character witnesses and close relatives who were all paid or brainwashed to testify in favor the indicted Klansmen.

Joan Doar warned the jurors that their opinions will forever remain perpetuated in the annals of history, so they should be careful about what side they take today.

On October 20, 1967, the court finally reached a verdict and eight defendants were found guilty. Sheriff Cecil Price and Imperial Wizard Sam Bowers were among those who were sentenced by the court. Rainey and Olen Burrage were not found guilty and were able to escape from the tight noose around their necks. Edgar Ray Killen was also acquitted as the court could not reach a verdict in his case.

Forty years after the crime happened, Ray Killen was finally charged with three counts of murder. He was found to be an accomplice to murder as he was the mastermind behind the conspiracy that led to the deaths of the civil rights activists. He was sentenced to 60 years in prison. The grand jury was still unable to sentence the remaining seven members of the Ku Klux Klan linked to the Mississippi attacks.

After an interview with Sam Bowers, the Ku Klux Klan Imperial Wizard at the time the murders took place, the case was revisited by the judicial system. Sam Bowers showed no remorse and said that he was delighted with his decision to help out his fellow Ku Klux Klan associates who carried out the attacks on his orders.

Bowers also said that Killen was the main man behind the attack. Killen assembled the lynch mob that murdered Schwerner and his friends in cold blood. People like Bowers were the main reason behind the plague that engulfed Mississippi and its residents. They instilled hate in the minds of the people and segregated them for the sake of his own racist agenda. The Klu Klux Klan is still active in different regions of the United States and still continues to instigate such crimes against the minorities. The Klu Klux Klan believes that white people have been gifted with the God-given right to kill anyone who stands against them.

The prejudiced attitude of the state of Mississippi in the murders of Schwerner, Chaney and Goodman was a stepping stone for civil rights activists to unify and work together so that such incidents no longer happen in any part of the country. A tragedy that was supposed to subdue the black community backfired and provided the black people an added incentive to fight for their rights. This is proof that African Americans are a resilient community and it takes more than a terrorist hate group to bog them down. Despite the atrocities inflicted on their black brothers, they still fearlessly trod on and made a place for themselves in the unfavorable hate-fueled environment of Mississippi.

Despite the resolve shown by the black community, the murders haunted them for decades and taint the image of this southern state to this very day. That's the thing about history. It never forgets. It's true that delayed justice is no justice at all. Even though Killen was sentenced for his crimes, justice did not prevail. He should have been punished for his crimes in the year he committed the crime. He should not have been allowed to roam around in society to spread further hate and violence. Many of the Klansmen got away with what they did. This shows the ineffectual nature of the judicial system.

*Farm outside Philadelphia, Mississippi, where the
FBI uncovered the bodies of Schwerner, Chaney,
and Goodman.
The buried bodies. Credit: FBI*

4.2 The KKK

The KKK, Facts, Beliefs, Violent History and the Future of the Klan

The Ku Klux Klan's violent history can be traced back to the late 19th century. The KKK has faced certain ups and downs, but it has always managed to survive and propagate its racist propaganda. This white supremacist terrorist organization is responsible for the dissemination of racism in different regions of the United States. The Ku Klux Klan is comprised of four to five thousand members, with accomplices in different spheres, advocates and sympathizers, who continue to spread its message of hate and corrupt the masses. It has the honor of being America's very first recognized terrorist organization, notorious for carrying out its heinous operations in ghostly uniforms.

Many forces, over the years, have tried to impede the progression of them, but it has shown great resolve and fortitude to preserve its existence. This resilience has made it a go-to organization for white people who are living in abject poverty. The KKK is the voice of these people. The Klan has made successful attempts to manipulate these downtrodden white people by listening to their desperate cries for help in times of social and political stress and used their weakness for their own advantage. The secret society is an organization filled with diabolical villains who have always found a way to blame their dissidents for their irrevocable mistakes and savagery. Its promise of empowerment of the poor has ulterior motives, and people are too naïve to understand that.

Klan march in Ashland, Oregon, 1920
Credit: The Oregon Encyclopedia

Enemies of the KKK

Who are the people who oppose the KKK? Well, groups that are affected most by the activities of the KKK, i.e., minorities who compete with white supremacists for jobs and an honorable place in society and the political system, are the ones who stand against the them and their racist regime. These minority groups include religious groups, African Americans, immigrants, LGBT communities, etc.

Klansmen are no different than their leaders and have a knack for treating themselves as victims whenever things get a little bit dirty. They try to defend their ideology with twisted reasoning and logic. They think that their lifestyle is threatened by minority groups and they have an obligation to do whatever is necessary to protect themselves and their way of life from an enemy that is not even remotely violent and only competes with the white supremacists on the basis of merit. There is a sense of deniability embedded in the hearts of the KKK members. They think that they have been blessed with a God-given right to declare war on people who threaten their ideology.

Important Things to Know about the KKK

This group has been around since the last days of the Civil War, but there are so many things that we don't know about this ancient terrorist organization. The terrorist group was originally formed by college students. It started off as a harmless prank and later grew into a full-fledged terrorist organization and a preeminent hate group.

Nathan Forrest was the first leader, the Grand Wizard of the Klan, but he decided to disband the KKK after finding out that it was inciting people to enact violent crimes against the minorities in America. Some parts of the organization were still functioning, but the organization as a whole remained quiet for approximately 45 years.

After the release of the famous book, The Birth of a Nation, they underwent resurgence and rose from the ashes to unimaginable heights of violence and tyranny.

The Klan has a number of divisions, pointing to the fact that it's not just an ordinary organization, it's a well-thought-out concept. The subdivisions include realms, dominions, provinces and dens, and each subdivision has its leadership and members. Grand Dragons, Cyclopes, Titans and Giants are titles assigned to members holding leadership positions in the above mentioned KKK categories.

Daniel Burros was an amusingly eccentric member. He had a Jewish origin but decided to join the Klan nonetheless. He climbed the ranks swiftly and, in no time at all, attained the prestigious position of Grand Dragon of New York. Burros tried to hide his Jewish background from the KKK leadership, but a New York Times article revealed his secrets. He killed himself shortly after that, in front of a dozen witnesses.

Klan members can be easily recognized due to their pointy hoods and white ghost-like uniforms. They also carry a burning cross. However this habit of carrying around a burning cross was adopted, it wasn't something that members of the original organization did. This burning cross was courtesy of the book, "The Birth of a Nation" based on the controversial novel, The Klansmen, written by Thomas Dixon. Dixon, inspired by Sir Walter Scott, decided to include the picture of a burning cross after he read the poem, The Lady of the Lake. The poem told tales of a forgotten Scottish tradition of burning a cross whenever a meeting was to be called.

The KKK Organization

In the early years of the twentieth century, the Ku Klux Klan had independently branched out and built strongholds in different parts of the United States. There are a total of 110 Klan groups that work independently. However, there are some that enjoy a prestigious affiliation with national organizations.

These national organizations are run by Imperial Wizards who are worshipped like gods by the members. There is a subdivision of the larger Klan groups known as a Realm that carries out its affairs within a state or regional collection of states. They have a single powerful leader possessed with an indomitable spirit and a powerful personality who is responsible for the development of the organization and makes major

135

decisions that pave the way for the future.

Outdated Doctrines

In the beginning of the twenty-first century, there were two types of Klansmen. One type followed the doctrines and teachings of David Duke. David Duke is a highly respected name in the history of the Ku Klux Klan and took command of the Klan in the 1970s. He revolutionized the way the Klan worked. He encouraged the followers of the Klan to run for office and cease the ancient and outmoded practice of burning crosses like uncivilized savages. Duke converted the Ku Klux Klan into something that came close to social acceptance. Duke was a master politician and knew how to play with words. Instead of speaking in a direct acrimonious tone that easily revealed his racist mentality, he opted to use euphemisms for racial slurs for diplomatic reasons. The Klansmen followed in the footsteps of their leader and took pride in their history and legacy instead of admitting their deep-rooted hate for other groups.

The other type was bold and fearless. They didn't care about what people thought of them and had total apathy for the consequences of their actions. They took pride in the Klan's heritage as a terrorist group. They rebuked law enforcement agencies openly and had no intention of concealing their beliefs.

Ku Klux Klan's Fundamental Ideology

The school of thought of the scattered Ku Klux Klan of contemporary times has evolved. The members no longer adopt only two stances. There are a wide range of doctrines and beliefs that are being followed by associates in recent times. The ideology has been broken down into subcategories: religious, political, racial, and anti-Semitic beliefs. However, this classification may vary from one member to another.

The fundamental ideology of the Klan is that white privileged Americans are under threat from minorities who can cause a shift of power from white Americans to minority groups. The conspirators who are sponsoring this movement against the Klan are Jews, according to the founders of the KKK. According to this ideology, it is the duty of the Klan members to unify and strengthen themselves against enemy forces to protect white America.

A common assumption in their ideology is that immigrants and non-whites compete with whites and pose a threat to their supremacy. Therefore, Klan members must take effective and immediate action to eliminate these threats through direct confrontation or through the aid of the government. However, when the government does not comply with the requests of the KKK, the Klan starts to treat the government as a hurdle in their path.

Political issues that the Klan shows involvement in include immigration issues, foreign relations, gun control laws, etc. The Klan firmly believes in an America ruled by the white population, an America that has no place for anyone but white Americans. In matters of immigration, the KKK has strongly suggested that the military should be deployed on U.S. borders to stop the increasing influx of immigrants on American shores.

Retrieving America back from the filthy and unwarranted grasp of minority groups is one of the key points of the Klan ideology. The Klan believes that foreign forces that do not belong in the United States are colluding against America and trying to demolish its true identity. A syndicate of religious fanatics, socialists, gays and other minorities has taken control of the government, according to this racist group. The KKK has vowed to fight against these forces and restore America to its former glory.

How are KKK members recruited?

The recruitment structure of the Klan is systematic and well organized. A Kleagle bears the responsibility of incorporating new Klan members into the hate group. These new additions are termed as Ghouls. The Kleagle gets a commission in return for his services. In the 1940s, each new member was obligated to pay a fee of 10 dollars and an additional annual payment of 6.8 dollars.

The organization has taken advantage of devastating attacks including the brutal massacre in June 2015 in South Carolina. The motive behind their involvement after the attack was the recruitment of new talent. During the summer of 2015, the Klan promoted itself by distributing fliers, telephone numbers, and their website address to let people know that the Klan is recruiting new members. According to reports, most of the potential candidates of the Klan membership have a criminal background or are presumed to become criminals in the imminent future.

Another recruitment policy employed by the Klan is advertisement through the web. Thomas Rob, who is the current head of the KKK, spreads word about the terrorist organization and hate group in a show called The Klan on his website. Other shows are also shown on the same website and shows like The Andrew Show are broadcast on YouTube. There is a separate show exclusively aired for white women called The Women's Perspective. All these sources are used to advertise and to recruit members from all age groups.

Violent Activities

The group has a history of orchestrating

violent attacks on the general population. The Ku Klux Klan instilled fear in the minds of the people by targeting non-whites in violent attacks including rape, lynchings and other despicable crimes on the minorities during the Reconstruction era. The KKK has tried to establish white authority through intimidation and fear since olden times. They are well known for lynching black people in front of a mob, without any proper trial, in the presence of a judge. Their hands have always been dirty with cold-blooded murder, whether they accept it or not. A cataclysmic upheaval of lynchings occurred during the 1920s, and by 1930, more than 4,000 African American were lynched by the racist and tyrannical organization, the Ku Klux Klan.

June 21, 1964: Abetted by the Deputy Sheriff in Philadelphia, Mississippi, police and Klan members brutally battered innocent black men and then murdered three civil right workers in cold blood.

November 3, 1979: The Death of the Klan march was raided by KKK scoundrels, and five civil rights activists were killed by them with the assistance of American Nazi Party associates.

March 1981: Michael Donald, a teenager and student, was lynched by two members of the KKK, and one of the assailants was later sentenced to death and executed in 1997.

April 1997: Police arrested four Klan

members for allegedly planning terrorist attacks in North Texas. After inquiry, they were found guilty of multiple crimes.

August 2005: Daniel James Schertz confessed to his crimes and pled guilty for making pipe bombs that were going to be used to cause explosions in buses transporting Mexican and Haitian workers from Tennessee to Florida.

May 6, 2010: A KKK leader by the name of Raymond Foster was found guilty of shooting and killing Cynthia Lynch who was thinking of leaving the Klan.

May 15, 2014: Steven Dinkle, a prominent member of the Ku Klux Klan, was sentenced to two years in prison on account of obstruction of justice and hate crime.

April 13, 2014: A senior leader of the KKK Frazier Glen Cross, Jr., killed three Jewish Americans in community centers not so far from Kansas City.

June 2015: Black Catholics were murdered by Dylan Roof, a white supremacist scum. Not so long after that, the Valiant White Knights of the KKK disseminated their lies and propaganda in the form of candy packets to the citizens of different cities.

November 11, 2015: Frazier Glenn Cross, Jr., egregious for his intense hatred for the Jews was found guilty of capital murder. He was also convicted on charges of attempted murder on three different occasions. He showed no remorse when he was sentenced to death and screamed 'Heil Hitler' upon hearing the verdict.

Stern Opposition against the KKK

The KKK faced considerable pressure from African Americans and other minority groups. In 1953, Horace Carter and Willard Cole were honored for their public services. They succeeded in reducing Ku Klux Klan numbers in their communities, despite the constant death threats. They put their lives and the lives of their families in danger to put more than 100 Ku Klux Klan members behinds bars. They were awarded the Pulitzer Prize for Public Service for their valiant efforts.

The Battle of Hayes Pond was a humiliating endeavor in the history of the KKK. They threatened two Lumbee Native American families by burning crosses at their homes, and the Lumbee Native Americans responded with force. They surrounded many members during a nighttime rally and killed many KKK members in an onslaught and forced them to retreat.

The approach of the FBI towards the Klan was confounding. Although the FBI had planted spies in the organization to monitor their activities, their main motive behind this infiltration was to look out for any communist link within the KKK. They did not pay much attention to the Klan's involvement in crimes against the minorities. However, in 1964, FBI launched a program with the code name COINTELPRO which directed its efforts to dismantle terrorist civil rights organizations such as the KKK.

The Klan Act and the Enforcement Act from the olden days were reinstated and were used to indict and prosecute Klan members.

The in-depth investigation of the House Un-American Activities Committee laid out the criminal methods and the horrendous picture of the entire KKK before the public.

The Branching out of the KKK in countries other than the United States

The KKK has tried to extend its reach many times. It has tried to place its feet in countries outside the United States countless times. There is a Ku Klux Klan currently operating in Canada, and it is flourishing.

Peter Coleman, formerly a One Nation member, tried to put KKK's roots in Australia in the 1990s. The Klan has also tried to make its way into the Australian political system in recent years. Some reports have suggested that some of the members are already a part of certain political parties in Australia.

The Klan has also made its way into the United Kingdom, and according to some reports, Robert Relf was allegedly involved in the establishment of a British Klan organization.

The European White Knights in Germany have drawn some attention after their emergence. In 2012, two police officers who were members of the German organization were allowed to be a part of the police force despite their membership in the KKK.

The Ku Klux Klan was also able to reach as far as Fiji in the 1870s. White settlers from foreign lands established a Klan to protect their interests, but when British colonials found out that they had plans to rebel against the crown, they eradicated its existence in Fiji, putting an end to the evil of the KKK in Fiji forever.

A Klan website was launched in Brazil by a group called Imperial Klans, and shortly after its launch, the leader of the Imperial Klans was apprehended and placed into police custody.

What does the Future hold for the KKK?

Despite facing severe resistance and opposition from the public and the government, the Ku Klux Klan still stands tall. Though it does not enjoy the same notoriety and power it did back in the 1920s and in the '50s and '60s, it is still the most widespread terrorist hate group in the United States.

The future of the Ku Klux Klan seems bleak. Further decentralization will hit the higher Klan organizations like a truck. However, smaller Klan groups, working independently, might be able to weather this storm. However, they will not have the same support and funding as they did before. New hybrid Klan groups might also come into existence, concocted by the collaboration of Neo Nazis and Ku Klux Klan members. Both of them share similar interests and might join hands to strengthen themselves and support each other. Klan criminal activity isn't likely to decline in the future.

5. White Collar Crimes

5.1 Enron

What is Enron? Who Were the People Behind This Giant Corporation?

Enron Corporation was an American company located in Houston, Texas, whose eventual fate was bankruptcy. It was formed as a result of a merger in 1985 between Houston Gas Co. and InterNorth Inc., when the deregulation of energy created an opportunity for a business such as this one. Enron quickly developed itself into an energy trader and supplier, eventually becoming well established and renowned as "America's Most Innovative Company" by Fortune magazine for six years.

Most of Enron's higher hierarchy came from humble backgrounds. They were overly ambitious and were willing to do whatever it took to make their way into the crème de la crème of the corporate world. They shared similar views and had personality traits that didn't differ considerably. The chairman of Enron, Ken Lay, was the son of a preacher, and he had lived in poverty his entire life. Living in such abject conditions corrupts your morality. Lay wanted to change his life and he dreamt of big things. He wanted to be the Kingpin of the corporate world. He earned his Ph.D. in economics from a prestigious institute. Another one of the executives of Enron, Sharon Watkins, had a similar childhood. She was brought up by her single mother who inspired her to get a Master's degree in accounting and she did.

The managers and executives in Enron were hardworking and astute and knew how to deal with tight situations and how to work around them. According to Schwartz and Watkins, the management team devoted 80 hours a week to the company. One of the most intellectually gifted members of the Enron management was Cliff Baxter, who adopted the title of vice chairman after joining Enron. He was exceptional at cutting deals.

All geniuses, however, have their monsters, and Baxter's monster was depression. After the company filed for bankruptcy, Baxter committed suicide. Jeffrey Skilling, another financial prodigy springing from the prestigious university of Harvard, was the chief operations officer at Enron. He was teased by his friends and colleagues for being a nerd, but through great resolve and tenacity, he changed his entire image and became a fashionable individual with a charismatic personality. This happened after his divorce. He decided that he would no longer be bullied by people and changed the way he was perceived by others.

Enron was the central hub of corruption in California. It exploited the citizens of California and looted them. Enron had some conflicts with the local companies when a power station in India was shut down out of the blue.

These disagreements with the local companies reflect the nature of the company and the way it was run. The citizens of California invested a lot in Enron in the form of taxes, pensions and savings, and they lost everything.

The Meteoric Rise of Enron

When Samuel Segner, the CEO of the newly formed company, resigned, Kenneth Lay took the throne. It was then named Enteron and was later shortened to Enron. Though it did not start off with profits, Enron, during its first year, suffered a loss of around $14 million. Then in subsequent years, by 1992 it became well enough established to earn around $122 billion from its gas contracts.

During the first few years it operated as a traditional gas supplier, but because it had to fight off the burdensome debt and battle a hostile takeover, everything changed once the American government policy allowed market deregulation in regards to the natural gas industry. Enron fed off the governmental policy, allowing consumers increased access over pipelines. Because the supply rose, the prices for natural gas were reduced over 50% between the period of 1985 to 1991. It also charged other firms using its pipelines, and it was able to use other companies' pipelines for transporting gas.

Jeffrey Skilling started working for Enron around this time period and was able to convince the board that the business needed a forward market for the gas sector. He did this by setting up a "gas bank" which helped created an intermediary for gas supplies, purchase and selling, and deliveries of gas. Kenneth Lay bought the idea of Skilling, attracted by the possibility of forward contracts which would be tempting to the consumers due to reduction in risk of price fluctuation. It soon became a success, allowing Enron to buy and sell gas derivatives and earn surplus from charging a fee for supplying the market with liquidity.

By 1990, Enron started diving into other areas and sectors of the energy market, such as coal, fossil fuels, electricity, water plants, pulp and paper production and broadband. Due to the success of the business, Enron became inspired enough to establish a broadband network for trading bandwidth. Skilling had introduced the "asset light" strategy and based its operations around it. Enron was trading internationally by this time and had established a huge plant at Teesside in the UK, with a contract to build another in Mumbai, India. By this time, Skilling and Lay were persuading Washington to deregulate electricity and with high hopes took Enron to California and purchased a power plant on the west coast. But the deregulation in California didn't go as planned and in fact many of the international contracts were lost due to ineffective administration.

Enron's Practices

Removing debt from balance sheets allowed Enron to put a façade of prosperity and losses were covered up.

Enron could not adopt the asset light strategy in other areas of the business. It bought Portland General Electric and tried to divide the company and sell off the power plant. But this eventually failed and the business was sold with a $1.1 billion loss.

In 1997, Skilling became the CEO of Enron. In 1992, Skilling had suggested it used a mark-to-market accounting system which estimates future revenue when a contract is made. This means that the estimates were included in accounting records, even though no money had been made from these projects yet. So, in simple terms, investors were given misleading information due to the varying estimation.

Enron's mark-to-market practice as well as others made it difficult to see how Enron was actually making money. Though the revenue and numbers on the books were high, it didn't pay the relative high taxes. Basically, the accounting method allowed the business to make money without bringing in taxable cash.

Who Abetted Enron in this Scandal?

How was Enron able to conceal its debilitating financial condition from the alert eyes of financial regulation authorities? Well, Enron was abetted by banks who gave the company multimillion dollar loans that enabled Enron to use fraudulent accounting practices to hide these loans, and the worst part is that some banks were fully aware of what Enron was doing, so these banks can be considered as accomplices to the crime.

Enron was a ticking time bomb. It suffered from a crumbling hidden balance sheet. JP Morgan Chase, Citigroup Inc & Co. provided 8 billion dollars in loans to Enron with hefty fees and interest payments. These weren't the only banks that were doing business with Enron. Enron did financing deals worth a staggering 1 billion dollars with five other notable and reputable banks.

The value of the shares of Citigroup Inc & JP Morgan Chase plummeted drastically after these financing deals with Enron. The banks completely denied any link with Enron. The market value of these shares dropped exponentially.

The investigative subcommittee started a thorough investigation of Enron and left no stone unturned. They scrutinized countless documents and had tedious talks with the people who were connected to Enron in any possible way. The Wall Street investment banks were also dragged into this investigation to further understand the severity of the situation.

All of this was done by the banks because they were getting a fair share of profit in the form of interest payments and hefty fees.

If it were not for the support of the banks, Enron could never have done what it did. It could never have pulled off all those lies and financial deceptions. But the banks showed no signs of remorse at any point and wanted to exacerbate the situation by giving a hand to

Enron so that it could further broaden its horizons and spread its plague to new financial locations.

The investors were misguided by the banks. The banks gave Enron their vote of confidence whenever investors came to them for trades and financial dealings.

Confusing and sophisticated transactions were made to enhance the anemic flow of Enron to catch up with its profit growth, but only on paper.

The Downfall

When the telecom industry suffered its decline, Enron became distressed too. Thus, this triggered business analysts into finding out how Enron was making money. The Raptors were dependent on Enron's stock, so if it fell below a certain level, the Raptors would fall. Enron had created such a complex spiderweb of deals that no one could figure out the legality of these agreements. So eventually when the stock began to decline, the Raptors suffered a great collapse. In 2001, Jeffery Skilling resigned due to some personal family issue. The former CEO, Kenneth Lay, resumed his position as CEO.

Ethical Factors behind the Downfall of Enron

Lots of things went wrong with Enron, but ethically, Enron made personal mishaps, organizational blunders and had systematic problems. Personal causes were due to the sinister motives of the workers employed by Enron. The workers in Enron had been contaminated with greed and stopped following the direction of their moral compass and paid the price for it.

The mistakes made at organizational level were due to blunders in group activities. Groups have the power to influence their constituent members. Every member in a group has a moral obligation to stand against a decision if it breaches an ethical code. Groups not only affect how financial organizations work, but they can also influence entire civilizations.

Systematic factors pertain to external forces. These forces somehow played a part in the demise and rise of Enron. They include laws, financial regulation authorities, investment banks that did financing with Enron, social entities, etc.

Our legal and regulatory structure is outdated and flawed and has many loopholes that invites fraudulent companies such as

Enron.

Current laws enable companies like Arthur Andersen and give them the freedom to put in a vote of confidence for a company such as Enron, even though they are well aware of its crumbling financial state. They can hold consulting sessions and mislead investment bankers into believing that their investment is going to the right place.

Enron is a private company and its auditors are employed by the company itself. Why would these auditors do anything that would hurt the people who are employing them? They would be out of jobs. Therefore, they hesitate when it comes to sending out a report that can hurt the financial integrity of the company.

Giant firms like Enron have the necessary resources to manage employee pension funds by themselves. The law gives them permission to do so as well. There is a possibility that a private firm will abuse its power and use these funds in a way that benefits the firm but hurts the employees. Giving such power to a firm can wreak havoc for the employees, and that is what happened in the case of Enron.

Believe it or not, companies like Enron have their own twisted ethical values that prohibit managers and executives to interact or do business with a firm that is already in business with them. However, these ethical codes are just for show and can be deemed inadmissible by the board of directors. Our legal system gives managers the incentive to be part of arrangements where there is a conflict of interest. The managers are aware of the fact that they have to do whatever is best for the company, but the law further advocates them by stipulating that managers and executives are permitted to exercise their own business judgment, keeping in mind the best interests of the company.

Enron gained popularity in the 1990s. During the 1990s, the stock market skyrocketed. Start-ups were rolling in profits, businesses enjoyed a meteoric rise, consumers were emptying their pockets, and it seemed as if everyone was becoming filthy rich, but the truth was far more disturbing. In times like these, human avariciousness shrouds human morality. This is what happened to Enron as well. They thought that if everyone was making easy money, why should they be the ones who are left out? This "Profit Booming phenomenon" took the U.S. by storm, and Enron thought that as long as they were making profits, it didn't matter what path they had to take to achieve their goals.

Fraud Allegations

On August 15, 2001, Sharon Watkins, who was the vice president for corporate development, wrote a letter to Kenneth Lay, implying that Skilling had simply resigned because of accounting and illegal practices. In the letter she had stated, "I am incredibly nervous that we will implode in a wave of accounting scandals."

Around the same month, Chung Wu, a broker in Houston, emailed 73 clients and investors of Enron, warning them that Enron was in trouble and they should sell their shares.

Watkins contacted a friend working for Arthur Andersen, the accounting firm. He created a memo that addressed the point Watkins had raised. Watkins then met Lay in person and gave him a detailed six-page letter about the issues with Enron's accounting records. Lay asked whether she had told anyone about this and then promised that a law firm would review the issues raised. The firm established that nothing was wrong with the accounts since Andersen had himself approved of them.

Watkins had found out that SPEs were controlled by CFO of Enron, Andrew Fastow, and he and other employees made money and left Enron to the support of Raptors. As the stock crashed, the financial statements of Enron also suffered. Around October 16, Enron announced a loss of $618 million, then during the year stock fell drastically from $86 to 30 cents.

On October 22, the SEC began to investigate and dig into Enron's accounting procedures and the relevant partnerships. Then around November, the officials confessed to overstating the revenue and earnings by $57 million from 1997 to 2001. The business then declared bankruptcy in December 2001.

Following the declaration of bankruptcy of the mighty Enron, around 21,000 employees suffered, and in the subsequent four years, shareholders suffered the tragic loss of around $74 billion, of which $40-$45 million could be accounted to fraud. Twenty thousand employees won a suit against Enron and received around $85 million for around $2 billion worth of pension funds.

A lot of people lost their jobs, and security and their futures were compromised due to this.

Conviction

Andrew Fastow, who was the main man behind those complex deals, was convicted for

778 counts of fraud, conspiracy and money laundering. He accepted a plea bargain, sentenced to 10 years of prison and made to pay around $23.8 million; in exchange he had to testify against the company's officials.

Kenneth Lay and Jeffery Skilling were both indicted in 2004 for fraud. Lay was convicted for 6 counts of conspiracy and fraud while Skilling was convicted for 19 counts of fraud, conspiracy, false statements and insider trading. Lay died of a heart attack in 2006, but Skilling was sentenced to 24 years in prison.

Though in the beginning the business did not start off with unethical practices, the greed eventually led to the collapse of a giant energy company. Unethical actions were practiced by both executives and traders, and employees were driven to work unethically to raise stock prices because they were also paid in stocks.

After this renowned fraudulent exposure, the U.S. Congress passed the Sarbanes-Oxley Act which contained standards for public company boards, management and accounting firms.

The decline of Enron was caused by several factors, namely mark-to-market accounting method, and Special Purpose Entities. The people behind the operations of this business are also at fault, like Lay, Skilling, and Fastow. The scandal had widespread effects, rippling not only to those 21,000 employees but throughout the entire country of America.

Thousands of Americans were unemployed and lost their pensions in the Enron scandal. The Enron scandal did not just cause financial damage. The public and the investment companies at large lost their trust in the financial system.

The Sarbanes-Oxley Act was introduced which caused financial problems for many firms. They had to spend a lot to fulfill the accounting regulations mentioned in the Sarbanes-Oxley Act. Although the revamping was an absolute necessity and yielded positive results, it was still a pretty expensive endeavor for the companies.

Auditors have a big role in the Enron Scandal, and they did their part to further promote the unethical operations going on in Enron. Though some transactions were out of their reach, other financing activities that could be curtailed and reported by them were instead condoned.

Everything that happened at Enron indicates that it wasn't just the result of minor negligence or simply bad management. It was a deliberate sham contrived by people who were knee deep in corruption and fraud. The executives pulled out millions prior to the collapse of the corporation, and this greedy behavior makes the situation even worse.

There were convictions and prison sentences given to the executives, but the damage that has been done is permanent and irreversible. The public no longer puts their faith in a firm's financial statements. There is always a hint of uncertainty and doubt in their minds. The world of corporations has faced a major blow due to the Enron scandal. Enron's name will never be forgotten and will forever be recalled from the annals of the past whenever someone is defrauded by firms. Something of this magnitude will change the way the businesses work in the future.

5.2 Hurricane Katrina Fraud

An Opportunity for Making Money?

We all know how deadly Hurricane Katrina was -- the adverse consequences ranged from destroyed infrastructure to millions of fatalities of humans and animals. The losses are numerous and debilitating, rendering any sane person to lose their will to live.

The hurricane that caused an uproar and shook the civilians, as well as the social media platform, occurred on the morning of August 29, 2005. The storm brewing in the Bahamas was heading straight for the Gulf Coast states and fortunately the meteorologists predicted its path in time for civilians to be evacuated.

New Orleans, in particular, was in great peril because, for the most part, it is surrounded by water and the majority of it lies below sea level. The mayor of New Orleans, Ray Nagin, ordered immediate evacuation just one day before the storm hit. The tropical cyclone reigned from Florida to Texas, leaving destruction and death in its wake. The water reached some 6 to 12 miles from the beach, and this storm was labeled the third most intense tropical cyclone to reach landfall in the United States.

Situation of the city as the storm hits- people forced to move up to their attics.

Embankments had been built upon the river and lake surrounding New Orleans during the course of the twentieth century in order to prevent the city from flooding. Some of these levees were better built than others. However, nobody had expected them to completely collapse. As the storm hit, water gushed into the city, and by 9 a.m., all areas with low elevation were flooded with so much water that people had to crawl up to their attics to remain safe. As the day went on, almost 80 percent of the city was under some amount of water.

People of the city came together and acted bravely to help each other. Many distributed food and provided shelter to those who had nowhere to go. However, the government seemed to have been caught off guard as not enough preparations had been made. The federal government in particular had no solid plan to deal with the disaster. The president had no knowledge about how many houses and buildings had been wrecked by the flood or how much food and aid was required by the victims living in shelters.

According to the mayor's orders, thousands of people who were unable to make it out of the city were seeking refuge in the Superdome stadium in New Orleans, but food stocks were limited and people were left helpless.

All those who were not present at the stadium were in even worse conditions, they had neither food nor safety. These people fled to the Ernest N. Morial Convention Center complex, but even there, they faced nothing but disappointment.

The hurricane took a total of 2,000 lives and left the already poor citizens homeless and jobless.

The FBI

The special agent in charge, Ken Kaiser from Boston, was appointed as the on-scene tactical commander. He reported that more than 80 percent of the city of New Orleans was flooded with water, reaching rooftops in several areas.

Kaiser was responsible for leading a team of over 200 specially trained FBI agents, several rescue team members, helicopter pilots and other specialized personnel. The FBI took over the Law Enforcement Coordination Center, and an agency called The Task Force recruited members from various other agencies and were made responsible for various duties. Their foremost duty was to ensure security in the city. They worked to answer emergency calls, stop the burgling and the looting and took part in search and rescue missions.

The FBI command center was established at a downtown hotel that had been safe from severe flooding. The teams watched over the ruined city and guarded all important locations, including the destructed New Orleans FBI office. Police officers and FBI agents stayed in the downtown command center to secure confidential records, evidence and artillery, despite the rising water levels.

Disasters and frauds go hand in hand. Every time there is a disaster, there are countless people who file false cases for financial assistance and try to scam the government, as at a time like this. The government does not keep a detailed record of the money that is given out, thereby giving people a chance to exploit relief programs. It was seen when Hurricane Andrew flooded Florida, and it was seen yet again during the time of Hurricane Katrina. The total number of frauds will probably never be known, but more than 600 such fraudulent individuals have been charged. What's to notice here is that these scammers were spread over 22 states. Making the hurricane a 'national phenomenon', according to David Dugas, who is the U.S. Attorney in Baton Rouge.

The most common fraud schemes include identity theft, claiming to be victims, overcharging the government, using fake Social Security numbers or of those who have passed away.

Fraud

Amongst the cases reported to the task

force is that of Tina Marie Winston from Illinois who claimed to be a mother of daughters aged 5 and 6 whom she saw drown in the flood water. She also said that the flood had destroyed her home in New Orleans. The reality, however, was far from what was being told. It was found that the woman had no children and she lived very far away from the area where Katrina had struck. Although the judge took into account Winston's mental instability, she was, nevertheless, punished with four years in prison for fraud.

False auctions were held online for various items such as motorcycles. People were given the impression that the proceedings from the auctions would be donated to victims of Hurricane Katrina. However, these items were never given out to the winners. Two Romanian nationals were found guilty of helping to set up this fake auction. The losses in this case were found to be more than 150,000 dollars.

What's even more unfortunate is the fact that even police officials tried to scam the government. A former police chief of Independence and a former captain from Louisiana were found guilty of overcharging FEMA for the extra hours they worked and the amount spent on their vehicles after Katrina hit.

In Alabama, a woman named Lawanda Williams used fake names and Social Security numbers and managed to fraudulently collect

$277,377 in the name of losses she faced in Mississippi, Alabama, Louisiana and Florida. It was found that her home was not damaged by the flood and she used the money to buy property, a portable home, three cars and a 50-inch television! She has been found guilty and sentenced to 75 months of imprisonment. She will also have to pay back the amount she spent on the items she bought, according to court orders.

Jeffrey Alan Rothschild from Washington, D.C., pleaded guilty for attempting to collect more than $100,000 as a compensation for damage caused by the hurricane and admitting to being involved in other financial frauds. The man pretended to be someone else and used mailboxes in Florida, New York, Virginia and Tennessee to obtain 38 checks from FEMA. The court punished Jeffrey with eight-and-a-half years in prison for his crimes.

Before the hurricane hit the Gulf Coast, State Farm Fire and Casualty Company issued insurance policies that covered wind damages along with other things. As the hurricane hit, the company asked their claim adjusters to falsely classify wind damage as flood damage. This would prevent the company from having to pay hefty amounts to all policy holders and shift the financial burden onto the federal government. This fraud was reported by two sisters, Cori and Kerri Rigsby, who were working as claim adjusters in the company, under the law which allows citizens to claim frauds in place of the government while hiding their true identities from the organization. If the case is won, the citizens will get a share in the money that is to be returned by the company.

Plenty of other cases of fraud were also filed against State Farm. The state of Mississippi filed a lawsuit against the company saying that the company falsely claimed more than 522 million dollars from the state for its policy holders and avoided its own responsibilities through forging reports of its adjusters.

Three people from Mississippi were found guilty of changing information in official documents and charging the federal government with $716,677 for Katrina debris cleanup.

Robert and Chressye Wallace from New Orleans were charged by the court for illegal fund collections that were meant for the hurricane victims.

The Wallaces owned three properties, one of which had been burnt down by fire in 2004. However, Robert submitted applications to the National Flood Insurance Program saying that the house that was destroyed in the fire was under four feet of flood water and managed to acquire $72,000 from the government.

Wallace tried to grab even more money

from the government by claiming that a second house was his permanent residence and was able to receive $50,000 as compensation from Small Business Administration. Chressye Wallace followed these footsteps and falsely claimed to be residing in a house that was not her primary home, managing to receive $150,000 from Louisiana Road Home Funds.

Robert Wallace has been charged with up to 20 years of jail time and a $500,000 fine while Chressye Wallace will have to face up to 10 years of imprisonment and a $250,000 fine.

Cheating the Charity

Devorah Goldburg of The Red Cross says that 104 people have been found guilty of cheating the charity and illegally claiming funds meant for the Katrina victims. 86 of these 104 criminals have been convicted, according to the spokesperson.

The majority of these scammers were found to be employees of the organization working at the Bakersfield call center on a contractual basis. Devorah stated that most of these people were responsible for approving cash payments to those affected by the hurricane. These workers schemed with their family and friends to file bogus cases and claimed funds.

The organization has been able to take

back 2.6 million dollars that were lost in cases of overcharging or claimed illegally by people. Seeing how seriously the organization had been carrying out investigations, a lot of money was returned in blank envelopes.

Erica Prince, recognized as the leader of this fraud scheme, teamed up with other people and filed 75 bogus cases to FEMA emergency assistance. She was caught when Social Security numbers and birthdates of 3 out of 8 people residing in apartments in Houston were found to be hers. The proceedings from this fraud were distributed amongst her, the person responsible for gathering information and the fake applicants. Through this scheme, Prince was able to claim 92,958 dollars as funds from FEMA until she was found guilty as charged. The court punished her with 33 months in federal prison while others were charged with shorter prison time and home detention.

While many people filed fake applications to claim funds, a lot of illegitimate charity programs were also created. These charities exploited kind-hearted people from across the country who wished to help those in need. In reality, these charities were fraudulent set-ups that did absolutely nothing to help the victims. An example of such fraud is the website called The Salvation Army International. The website was owned by two Texas brothers, Steven and

Bartholomew Stephens, who managed to gather the huge sum of 48,000 dollars before they were caught by authorities. Both brothers were pronounced guilty and imprisoned according to court orders.

Plenty of organizations associated with the federal government were also found guilty of fraud. The New Orleans Homeownership contractors overcharged the non-profit organization for the work they did to relocate people who had lost their homes. The previous head of the organization, Stacey Jackson, was also found to be involved in the fraud. She was sentenced to five years of imprisonment as punishment for her crime.

A subcontractor of sand and gravel was found guilty of scheming and taking bribes for the Army Corps of Engineers bids to build the New Orleans embankment. The subcontractor was charged with fraud and punished with five years of jail time.

Many politicians decided not to stay behind and watch others loot the government and were found to be involved in various frauds.

Some of these corrupt politicians include Sheriff Jiff Hingle who was found guilty of accepting 10,000 dollars from the construction company that was assigned the task of rebuilding local prisons that were destroyed by the hurricane. He also misused the money that was to be spent in campaigning. For these crimes, the sheriff was sentenced with three years and 10 months of imprisonment.

Councilman Joe Impastato was found guilty of asking for and being paid 40,000 dollars for brokering the contract signed by a Lacombe-based company for disposal of debris. He was also charged by the court for understating his income and was punished with 18 months of imprisonment.

Jon Johnson of New Orleans used the funds provided to his non-profit organization by FEMA for personal campaigning. He also filed an illegitimate application to the Small Business Administration and acquired money for his allegedly damaged home. He was declared guilty of his crimes and sentenced to six months in prison.

Many officials were found guilty of fraud when investigations were carried out by the task force. These officials include Benjamin L. Edwards, Sr., who was previously the director of the New Orleans sewerage. He was charged by the court for being involved in financial fraud, underpayment of taxes and for accepting 750,000 dollars from contractors assigned the task of cleaning up the city after the hurricane.

Another official who was charged by the court was the former mayor of Gulfport, Mississippi, Gregory Brent Warr who was found to be guilty of falsely claiming funds from the government that were meant for Katrina victims.

Danny Gene Hale claimed more than 10,000 dollars from FEMA as compensation for the damage caused to his house by the storm. In reality, it was found that Hale was not even living at his property for which he had received funds. Punishment sentences for Hale were passed by the district judge in southern Mississippi.

Joseph Pugh also faked his residency and received funds and food stocks illegally. He was sentenced to one year and one day of imprisonment and fined 12,107 dollars for his crimes.

Investigations carried out by the government in Louisiana found that 70 percent of the 1 billion dollars provided by Congress to Louisiana Road Home program for fixing and rebuilding homes to keep them safe from any future flooding were not accounted for. More than 24,000 people who claimed funds of 30,000 dollars each failed to show that the money had been utilized for repairing their damaged houses.

As the storm struck, money was handed out by FEMA and other organizations as funds for the victims. But countless cases of overcharging, falsely claimed money, and the like were uncovered through investigation. The fact that people managed to cheat the program makes it evident that the program has loopholes and is not as well protected as it should be.

Officials have ensured that safety checks have been established to prevent such cases in the future. FEMA said that most cases of fraud occurred through the telephonic system as it does not have enough security checks. The online system of filing application for funds has several security checks to prevent fraudulent money claims.

The Storm Passes but Problems Remain

Hurricane Katrina was one of the most intense catastrophic events to take place in the history of the United States. Apart from leaving hundreds and thousands dead, injured and homeless, the hurricane also played a huge role in revealing the conditions of the government support programs.

The government seemed unprepared and unaware of the severity of the situation and displayed a rather irresponsible attitude. It had formed no adequate plans other than evacuation. Thousands of people were left helpless, starving, and with nowhere to go as shelters and food supplies were limited.

The relief programs lacked security checks and were found to not be up to the mark, leaving opportunities to commit fraud. There was no follow-up on the money that had been paid to homeowners. People who were not eligible for funds received thousands of dollars while the deserving remained helpless.

The hurricane proved to be a serious wake-up call for the authorities to revise their system and come up with better, solid relief plans.

It is extremely unfortunate that corrupt individuals are found at every level -- from ordinary citizens to government officials, nobody spared the opportunity to put their hands in the cookie jar and loot the government during this predicament.

However, the work done by the Task Force to recover the money and sentence all those guilty proved that not all hope is lost. Millions of dollars were recovered and convicted criminals were punished for their crimes.

The silver lining of this tragic event was seen when the city came together in the time of need. The locals helped their neighbors in every possible way -- from distribution of food to offering shelters and rescuing individuals from drowning -- all efforts were made to ensure that the damage was minimized.

New Orleans was affected the most by Hurricane Katrina, and many people are still in the process of recovering from their losses, but the people are determined and the city marches on.

6. Terrorism

6.1 Anthrax Attacks

The whole of America had gone into a state of despondency and mourning after the terrible 9/11 terrorist attacks, and the government had just begun its War on Terror. The country was in shambles. One week after the 9/11 attacks, the U.S was hit with another vicious attack: the Anthrax Attacks. Beginning on September 18, 2001, people in the U.S. started receiving letters that contained anthrax spores. Five people died from these deadly attacks and 22 people became infected. In 2007, six years after the attacks, the FBI found out that the attacks were carried out by Dr. Bruce E. Ivins, but before the FBI could capture him, Dr. Ivins killed himself.

Introduction

The letters containing the spores were mailed over the course of three weeks. They were first sent on September 18, 2001, and again on October 9, three weeks after the first series of letters was mailed. The letters had come as a shock to the American government; they already had so much to fight against; just a week earlier, the 9/11 attacks had happened. Two planes, both of which had been hijacked by Al Qaeda terrorists, flew into the World

Trade Center and the Pentagon, respectively, and another plane, which had also been hijacked by an Al Qaeda terrorist, had crashed in Shanksville, Pennsylvania. Over 2,500 people had died in these attacks. America was already busy fighting a war against the Taliban; how were they going to defend themselves against the anthrax letters when they were already caught up in so many other things?

The letters were at first ignored and nobody even suspected that the disease was being caused because of them. Many people believed for some time that there was absolutely no connection between the disease and the letters. The U.S. dismissed it as a terrorist attack because they believed it was an isolated incident and would probably not happen again. Tommy G. Thompson, the Secretary of Health and Human Services at the time, said the U.S. had no evidence that this was an act of terrorism. And who would be so inept and paranoid as to call some letters a terrorist attack?

Many people had still not recovered from the state of shock they had been plunged into after the 9/11 attacks. They were not ready for another terrorist attack, so it was up to the government to soothe the fears of the people and remind them that the government was doing all it could to fight the perpetrators of the 9/11 attacks. Debbie Crane, a spokeswoman for the North Carolina Department of Health and Human Services, said, "Anthrax happens." For a very long time, the U.S. government kept denying that the disease was linked to the letters. People had nevertheless started seeking out Ciprofloxacin (an antibiotic that is used to treat anthrax). Their fears had already been aroused.

First Wave and USAMRIID's Involvement

It was not until Robert Stevens, a man who worked for American Media, Inc. (AMI), where one of the letters was sent, died from anthrax that the U.S. realized that this was much worse than they had initially thought. The first series contained five letters and they were mailed to: ABC News, CBS News, NBC News, The New York Post, and the National Enquirer at American Media, Inc. (AMI). Robert Stevens was the first person who died as a result of these attacks. Stevens, who worked at Sun (published by AMI) as a tabloid journalist in Boca Raton, Florida, died four days after getting infected. The letter contained anthrax in powdered form. It was believed that he had inhaled the powder. Stevens started exhibiting unusual behavior, and it was clear that his health was deteriorating. He was admitted to a hospital in Florida and his illness remained undiagnosed for some time; he died on October 5. The letters read:

"09-11-01

THIS IS NEXT

TAKE PENACILIN NOW

DEATH TO AMERICA

DEATH TO ISRAEL

ALLAH IS GREAT"

The victims' families of the anthrax attacks were excluded from the financial assistance that was being given to the 9/11 victims, so Robert Stevens's wife, Maureen Stevens, took it upon herself to file a lawsuit against the government, saying that the U.S. Army Medical Research Institute for Infectious Diseases (USAMRIID) had failed to keep the labs secure and their negligence had allowed the perpetrator of the anthrax attacks to get their hands on the Ames strain (one of the strains of the anthrax bacterium).

The September 11th Victim Compensation Fund, which provided the victims of the 9/11 attacks over $200,000, did not provide financial assistance to the victims of the anthrax attacks, and Maureen's lawyer believed that filing a lawsuit was her way of demanding money from a government who had failed to help her. The FBI did not have any clues at the time as to who had carried out the attacks, and many people thought that the attacks were linked to Al Qaeda terrorists since they had happened only a week after 9/11.

USAMRIID had become the center of attention during the investigations as many people started to believe that the anthrax in the letters might have been obtained from one of the labs of USAMRIID. Chuck Dasey, the spokesman of the Army, refused to say anything on the matter, and he only said that Maureen's claim that the anthrax had been obtained from Army's labs was only speculation and nothing more. How did USAMRIID get their hands on the Ames strain? Investigators had obtained it in Texas in 1981 from a dead cow, and it was sent to USAMRIID so they could conduct studies on it.

Amerithrax Investigations

Scientists all over the country were interrogated. The employees of USAMRIID were also questioned and a lie detector was used to check if they were telling the truth. The FBI believed that the anthrax could have been grown inside one of the labs of USAMRIID without authorization and then used in the attacks. Dr. Steven Hatfill, a scientist who used to work at USAMRIID, was considered the primary suspect by the FBI, and his house was searched. However, no evidence was found that suggested any connection between the anthrax attacker and the doctor. In 1992, it was discovered that someone was conducting experiments using anthrax in a lab at USAMRIID. It was also discovered that 27 samples, one of them being Ames anthrax, were lost, but the Army believed that the samples were completely harmless.

Richard Bieder believed that if it was proved that Ames could only be obtained from one of the labs of USAMRIID, then the Army was going to be put under a lot of pressure for letting down their guard and allowing the attacker to get their hands on the anthrax. However, if evidence was provided that suggested the existence of other labs harboring the anthrax, then it was possible to file a lawsuit against all of them and share the damages.

Robert Stevens was not diagnosed with anthrax until three or four hours after his death. According to his wife, he came home from his fishing trip and kissed her goodnight. Later, he started throwing up and said he could not breathe. He was taken to the hospital and was given a sedative after which he never woke up. It was believed that he might have inhaled it while fishing in North Carolina, but when AMI inspected his office, they found anthrax on his computer. The FBI was called as soon as possible and they termed the investigation "Amerithrax".

Second Wave of Letters and the Aftermath

On October 9, three weeks after the first wave, two more letters were mailed, this time to two Democratic Senators named Tom Daschle and Patrick Leahy. These letters read:

"09-11-01

YOU CAN NOT STOP US.

WE HAVE THIS ANTHRAX.

YOU DIE NOW.

ARE YOU AFRAID?

DEATH TO AMERICA

DEATH TO ISRAEL

ALLAH IS GREAT"

The letter that was mailed to Daschle was opened by a person working at his office. The letter written to Leahy, however, was sent to the wrong location because a ZIP code had been misread and it was not discovered until November 17th. The anthrax contained in these letters was believed to be much more harmful than the anthrax in the previous letters. Neither of the persons to whom the letters were directed came into direct contact with the anthrax and as a result were not hurt, but some of the people working at Daschle's office did. Moreover, the letter that was misrouted ended up killing two postal workers.

According to Grant Leslie, who opened the letter mailed to Daschle, the anthrax in the letters looked like "baby powder". Even though Leslie did come into contact with the anthrax, she was safe because she had taken antibiotics. However, 22 people contracted anthrax because of these attacks and five people died. After the death of the postal workers, the mail service had to be shut down. Some people believe that this is what finally forced businesses to use email. Many people still would not work with mail even after the postal services had resumed. People had started buying gloves so they would not come into contact with any disease that was stored inside the letters.

People working in the White House urged Robert Mueller, the FBI director, to blame Osama bin Laden for the letters, but he knew that people would never believe a lie as preposterous as that, so he refused. The anthrax that was used in the letters could only have been made using advanced scientific techniques; a person who hid in a cave in

Afghanistan could never have made something like this. Some people tried to put the blame on the government of Saddam Hussein while some people said that the attacks had probably been carried out by a single person who was most likely a scientist with access to labs containing advanced material.

After the letters that were sent to the two Democratic Senators, many fake letters were sent. The public, however, was not aware at the time that these letters were fake, and so they only served to aggravate the paranoia and the anxiety of the people. For example, a letter from St. Petersburg, Florida, and another letter from Malaysia were thought to be sent by the actual anthrax attacker, but they instead turned out to be fakes. The letter that was sent from Malaysia was connected to Dr. Steven Hatfill because his girlfriend was from Malaysia.

Another fake letter was sent to Daschle from London. The FBI tried to establish a link between Hatfill and this letter since he was in England when it was sent, but failed. Hatfill later sued the FBI for destroying his reputation. Because of these hoax letters, finding the actual culprit had proved to be a much more difficult task than the FBI had initially thought.

Further Investigations

When the anthrax used in the letter sent to Daschle was sent to the USAMRIID for investigation, it was discovered by a scientist named Peter Jahrling that it had silicon dissolved in it so the anthrax could easily enter and infect the lungs. When USAMRIID received the anthrax spores, they initially did not even completely know what they were looking for. They thought the spores had smallpox viruses in them. What the scientists tried to do, they put the spores under a Transmission Electron Microscope (TEM) and when they turned on an electron beam, they noticed that there was something oozing out of the spores. Jahrling was completely baffled when he made this discovery. According to author Richard Preston, when Jahrling saw this, he said out loud that there was something mixed in the spores and he believed that it might have come from Iraq or Al Qaeda.

After it was discovered that there were additives in the spores, Tom Geisbert, another scientist who worked at USAMRIID, ran a test on the anthrax found in the Daschle letter at Armed Forces Institute of Pathology (AFIP) and he found out that the spores contained silicon and oxygen. Since silicon dioxide is glass, it was deduced that the perpetrator had inserted silica in the anthrax. News was soon spread that the attacker had mixed deadly chemicals in the anthrax to cause as much harm as possible. This caused the FBI to believe that the mixture could only have been prepared by a single person who had great knowledge about scientific matters at their disposal. Thus, the possibility of it being a terrorist attack was finally ruled out. According to the scientists at USAMRIID, the attacker could have easily made the spores for $2,500, considering they had access to a laboratory.

Many newspapers had started spreading false reports, claiming that the material discovered in the anthrax spores was something that was not known to the scientists at USAMRIID. The FBI had suggested the spores were covered with fumed silica, but many people had doubted this theory. Many people started developing their own theories as to the composition of the material used in the letter. One person wrote in an issue of Science magazine, saying that the attacker might have used "polymerized glass" to attach silica to the anthrax spores.

Another article, titled "Forensic Application of Microbiological Culture Analysis to Identify Mail Intentionally Contaminated with Bacillus anthracis spores", written by Douglas Beecher for Applied and Environmental Microbiology, argued that the anthrax present in the letters did not contain any sort of additives and this was only a misconception spread by people who did not understand the composition of the powder. He said the dissemination of this misconception would only stand in the way of scientific advancement and would get in the way of research. In the same article, he also said that the spores were simply prepared through the method of purification. People argued that while the article had some good points, it failed to include too many authentic references and so could not be fully trusted.

Brian Ross, who worked as a journalist for ABC News, repeatedly claimed that the letter had been sent by Saddam Hussein's government. According to him, silica was not the only additive found in the spores when they were examined at Fort Detrick, Maryland. He argued that in addition to silica, there was bentonite in the anthrax, an additive which Saddam Hussein was very fond of and Iraq was the only country where bentonite was used. However, Scott Stanzel, a spokesman for the White House, said that nobody had found any bentonite in the anthrax. According to Major General John Parker, there was absolutely no possibility of there being a bentonite additive in the anthrax spores because they did not find any aluminum in them, only silica. How were they so sure that there was no bentonite in the spores? According to the Major, you needed both aluminum and a silicate to form bentonite, but since there was no aluminum in the spores, there was absolutely no way bentonite could have been found in them.

The Attacker Finally Gets Caught

FBI agents had been dispatched in six continents and they had conducted interviews with over 9,000 people. The FBI tried to establish a link between the anthrax attacker and the 9/11 attacks, but every evidence they had pointed to a scientist who worked at Fort Detrick. But, the evidence they had was not enough to land Bruce Edwards Ivins in court. Ivins had worked at Fort Detrick for over eighteen years, and many of the people who worked with him said that Ivins had neither the knowledge nor the skills to prepare an inhalable powder using anthrax. A colleague of Ivins stated that the FBI had carried out a raid on Ivins's home twice. According to him, Ivins was depressed and could not handle all the pressure the FBI had put on him.

In 2008, Jeffrey Taylor, U.S. Attorney for the District of Columbia, publicly claimed that Dr. Ivins was the only person who was responsible for creating the powdered anthrax.

Meryl Nass, an expert on biological warfare and anthrax, disputed his claim and said it was impossible to tell who the perpetrator is just from the spores; they could only be linked to a lab and a strain, but not to a single person. More than ten scientists worked at the laboratory from where the powdered anthrax was created. Moreover, workers from other laboratories in Ohio and New Mexico had access to the anthrax samples too. According to the FBI, there were 419 people in total at Fort Detrick who had the samples.

According to one of Ivins's therapists, Ivins had once threatened to poison a woman he was interested in. His therapist informed the police and the head of their clinic, but the police said that they could not do anything because they did not know who the woman was or where she lived. He also told the therapist that he "knew how to do things without people finding out".

In 2008, he told his new therapist that he had formulated a plan to kill the people who worked at his laboratory and "go out in a blaze of glory". According to the same therapist, even in Ivins's school days, he would threaten to kill people, and he exhibited very strange behavior. One of his psychiatrists, Dr. David Irwin, said Ivins was homicidal and that he exhibited the behavior of a sociopath.

According to the Department of Justice, Ivins was known to use samples from his laboratory without permission and would disinfect and clean the places where he had worked. Not only that, he also tried to put the blame on the people that worked with him. He was also known to be in possession of a book that contained secret codes which described methods that were very similar to those employed in the anthrax attacks. The Department of Justice had declared that Ivins was the only perpetrator. There was no one else who could have worked with anthrax like the one used in the letters. Ivins knew that the FBI had been trying to take him to court and he was already under a lot of psychological stress. On August 1, 2008, before the FBI could lay charges on him, Ivins killed himself by overdosing on Tylenol with codeine. It still remains unknown whether Ivins was actually responsible for the attacks or if the FBI accused him because of the pressure from the media.

6.2 Pan Am 103 Bombing

Overview

The Pan Am Flight 103 bombing was one of the most tragic, heart-wrenching and devastating events that has occurred in these terroristic times. What was supposed to be a normal flight take-off turned out to be of fatal consequence, one that resulted in the loss of hundreds of lives. Before we begin to reenact the details of this traumatizing event, let us all first take a moment to pray that history should never repeat itself again.

The flight was a daily scheduled transatlantic flight, hailing from Frankfurt to Detroit, and taking off from London to arrive at New York City. The flight took off on December 21, 1988, from London's Heathrow airport just four days before Christmas. This fact adds more pain, because one can only imagine, anticipating the arrival of a loved one for a family holiday, only to receive such devastating news of death by an exploding aircraft.

However, the aircraft did not explode due to mechanical failure but rather due to a bomb planted inside the aircraft, which killed around 259 people on board -- 243 passengers and 16 crew members. As the aircraft exploded mid-air less than 40 minutes (38 minutes to be exact) after the plane took off, the remnants and large ignited sections of the aircraft fell to the ground in a furious torrent, killing around 11 people on the ground. The plane exploded over a town named Lockerbie in Scotland, and until 9/11, this event became one of the most lethal and vile acts of terrorism as well as the most complex and sophisticated terrorist case to ever be investigated by the FBI.

Aircraft Details

The aircraft used for Pan AM Flight 103 was a Boeing 747-121. This was registered as N739PA and was named Clipper Maid of the Seas; it was previously named Clipper Morning Light. This plane was the 15th 747 of its kind and was delivered in February 1970, meaning its life span was only 18 years. It had journeyed over 75,000 flying hours. This aircraft even managed to gain some popularity for a short period of time as it aired on the fourth episode of Conquering the Atlantic of BBC Television series Diamonds in the Sky.

At around 6:25 p.m., the captain of Clipper Maid of the Seas, James Bruce MacQuarrie, was granted permission to take off from the control tower.

At 6:58 p.m., the co-pilot established contact with the Shanwick Oceanic Area Control situated in Ireland. This station is responsible for assigning flight corridors to aircraft flying over the North Atlantic so that collisions can be avoided.

After the station received the flight number, flying altitude and destination, the air traffic controller replied with 'Clipper 103 should take 59 north 10 west to Kennedy' at around 7:02 p.m. However, the station received no reply. Fifty seconds later, the air traffic controller saw the transponder's image vanish from the screen, and when the radar reported the position of the plane, the controller received images that astonished and horrified him -- the exploding Boeing aircraft that was disintegrating.

Assumptions of the Events

Since there were no survivors, we can only infer the events that unfolded during this horrid accident. The assumptions were based on facts that were gathered after the occurrence. Let us examine them meticulously for you. However, you must keep in mind that these are merely conclusions reconstructed after the event happened, the foundation of which is not concrete.

First there was an explosion that resounded throughout the aircraft and then as the electricity went out, the plane was encapsulated in utter darkness and desolateness. Then the fuselage at the front broke away mere seconds later and the nose of the plane detached itself and fell to the right side, down to a fatal crash. Now all the passengers and crew that were on board this decapitated plane experienced fatal cold, darkness and noise.

The air from the plane escaped and ice formed on the windows in a matter of mere seconds. The air became, thin, cold and harsh, causing people to lose consciousness. The main central body of the plane tilted forward, fragmented into several pieces, and began to plunge itself down below.

Passengers that were seated at the front were hurtled and catapulted forcefully out of the rupturing plane and out into the sky while some of the passengers were pulled into the engine that was still roaring at full throttle. However, many passengers were in two divisions of the plane that broke off and fell at a level that had warm air with oxygen. Though it is estimated 60 percent of those passengers were alive, no one knows if any one of them regained enough consciousness to further view the horrible and scary chain of events that occurred further into time as the plane continued to fall.

The explosion blasted a 20-inch hole in the left side of the fuselage, and the Federal Aviation Administrator inferred that no emergency procedures were started in the cockpit. The cockpit voice recorder that was found by police within 24 hours, contained no evidence of a distress signal, though a 180-millisecond hissing noise was heard as the explosion wrecked the communication center. The Air Accidents Branch of British Department of Transport reported that the nose of the plane had broken off from the main body within three seconds after the explosion occurred. It was sheared off but held on by a band of metal only briefly, until it eventually broke off, hitting the third engine and crashing near the church.

Factual Events

With the motors still running, the plane dropped in 36 seconds. However, the strong wind from the west meant that it did not crash straight onto the ground but rather dragged and drifted to fall on the town of Lockerbie. The wings and the fuselage, which held around 90 tons of kerosene, fell on Sherwood Crescent. The middle body of the aircraft with its wings, ripped the earth 47 meters long and 1 meter deep.

At Sherwood Crescent, houses situated between number 13 and 16 were completely destroyed, while several others were damaged beyond repair. A total of 21 buildings had to be torn down. An artificial knee was what remained of the eleven victims who died from the crash's impact.

The fiery craft reached a local gas station and its diesel tanks exploded. The four engines fell on either side of the railway track and a 20-meter piece of rear fuselage crashed at Rosebank Crescent while the front fuselage and the cockpit fell at a sheep pasture near Tundergarth church.

There were many other small components and parts of the plane that were raining from the sky and showering down to the earth in angry torrents. These included pieces of metal, damaged suitcases, whiskey bottles, seats and coins. These struck streets, houses, rooftops, and windows; even pages from books were found around 130 kilometers away.

Prior Warnings

Sixteen days prior to the attack, on December 5, Federal Aviation Administration delivered a security bulletin that said that a guy with an Arabic accent had phoned the U.S. Embassy in Helsinki, Finland. He informed that a Pan Am flight going from Frankfurt to the U.S. would be bombed within two weeks. This threat, so it was told, came from someone associated with Abu Nidal Organization and that a Finnish woman would act as an unwitting courier, carrying the bomb onto the flight.

Despite the fact that the warning was taken seriously by the U.S. government and the State Department relayed the information to various embassies, this unfortunate event still occurred. All U.S. carriers were informed, including Pan Am, which charged passengers about $5 for extra security measures involving screening of passengers, employees, baggage, facilities and aircraft, etc.

The Frankfurt security team found a paper which contained the warning under a pile of papers the day after the event occurred. The screener at Frankfurt responsible for detecting explosives under X-ray, told ABC News that she didn't know what Semtex was until 11 months after the bombing. Semtex is a plastic explosive and was one of the components that were used in the Pan Am 103 bombing.

The bombing technique, however, is discussed later. Two days after the bombing, the Finnish national newspaper, Hufvudstadsbladet, published on the front page that the spokesperson for the State Department, Phyllis Oakley, confirmed the threat to the Helsinki Embassy. The newspaper also stated that the voice related the fact that the bomb would journey from Frankfurt to New York on Pan Am's flight to the United States. The person carrying the bomb would be unaware that the explosive was hidden in their luggage, carrying death in their own hands.

Also, the newspaper in particular wrote that the man with the Arabic accent who allegedly phoned the embassy belonged to "Abu Nidal's radical Palestinian fraction" that is claimed to be involved in many terrorist activities and stated that the bomb would be carried on board by a woman.

Fatalities

This act of terrorist bombing resulted in a total of 270 deaths: 243 passengers, 16 crew members and 11 persons on the ground. The nationalities of these people consisted of 189 American citizens, 43 of British origins, and the remaining 21 were from various countries including, India, Hungary, Japan,

Argentina, Belgium, etc.

The Pan Am Boeing 747 Flight 103 was under the command of Captain James Bruce MacQuarrie, an experienced pilot who had accumulated over 11,000 flight hours. The co-pilot in command, the first officer or second pilot was Ray Wagner, who had over 5,500 hours flight experience, and the flight engineer, Jerry Don Avritt, had over 8,000 hours of working above ground and in the sky.

The Heathrow cabin pursers included the following members: Gerry Murphy, Milutin Velimirovič, attendants Siv Engström, Babette Avoyne-Clemens, Noëlle Campbell-Berti, Elke Kühne, Nieves Larracoechea, Irja Skabo, Paul Garrett, Lili Macalolooy, Jocelyn Reina, Myra Royal and Stacie Franklin.

The nationalities of these crew members ranged from Czechoslovakia, the Dominican Republic, France, Norway, Philippines, Spain, Sweden, West Germany, and United States.

Some of the first-class passengers, along with the pilot, co-pilot, flight engineer and an attendant were found still in the seats in the nose of the plane after the plane crashed in a field near a church in Tundergarth. It has been said that the flight attendant was hanging on for her dear life after the crash and was found by a farmer's wife, although she died shortly afterward, before the wife could summon help.

A pathologist also inferred that at least two of these passengers may have remained alive, albeit briefly, and might have survived the crash if they had been found sooner.

There were around 35 students from Syracuse University who were returning to their homes to enjoy Christmas holidays with their loved ones, but unfortunately, they never made it home from London and the anticipating families opened their doors to greet awful news.

Amongst the hundreds of passengers and travelers were these notable people as well. These included 50-year-old Bernt Carlsson who was the UN commissioner for Namibia; Volkswagen America CEO James Fuller, as well as the marketing director, Lou Marengo; a musician named Paul Jeffreys and his wife Rachel; Joanna Walton, a lyricist; Jonathan White, son of the actor David White; Alfred Hill, an aspiring promising physicist; and Irving Sigal.

On this devastating flight, some U.S. government officials were also travelling. At least four were confirmed to be on board while the fifth was never confirmed. This roused some conspiracy theories that one or more of them were the target of this sadistic bombing.

Not on Board

There were also some fortunate people who were supposed to be on that flight but were saved either by their tardiness or due to changed plans.

Amongst these very fortunate people was an Indian mechanic, Jaswant Basuta. He was a 47-year-old car mechanic who had booked a flight on Pan Am 103 but reached the boarding gate too late. He was supposed to go to New York to start a new job, but life had different plans for him that did not involve death on an exploding airplane. Initially he became a suspect as his baggage was on the flight and also because he was a Sikh. Three years ago, a Sikh militant was known to be involved in the bombing of Air India Flight 182. However, shortly after he was questioned at the Heathrow police station, he was released.

John Lydon, also known as Johnny Rotten, the lead singer and song writer of the popular band Sex Pistols, had also booked a ticket for himself and his wife on this unfortunate flight. He was lucky enough to be married to Nora Foster who made them miss their flight due to delays in packing. Mats Wilander, a renowned tennis player, also made a reservation but never boarded the plane.

Another person among these fortunate people was actress Kim Cattrall who went on a last-minute shopping binge and changed her reservation for the flight in time.

Bomb and Exploding Material

The FBI and DERA forensic teams ran an analysis on the deposits of carbon on containers AVE4041 and AVN7511 and concluded that the bombing occurred due to a chemical explosion with 12-16 ounce charges of plastic explosive that had been used and that it exploded around 8 inches from the left side of the container.

Upon examination of two metal strips from AVE 4041, Alan Feraday and Dr. Thomas Hayes of the DERA were able to discover traces of both pentaerythritoltetranitrate and cyclotrimethylenetrinitramine, components of Semtex-H. Semtex-H is a high-functioning plastic explosive that was made in Czechoslovakia. Later in March 1990, it was informed by the Czech president that a former communist regime had supplied a large amount of Semtex to the government of Libya via a company named Omnipol.

Investigation

It didn't take much time for the investigation process to begin. On December 21, around 7 p.m., the local Procurator Fiscal (public prosecutor) had already started working on the case. Police officers were sent to Lockerbie in Dumfries and Galloway where the debris of the plane had fallen. However, it was soon found that the Scottish police officers of Dumfries and Galloway did not have the proper resources that were required to investigate a case of this magnitude. Soon enough, the Dumfries and Galloway Constabulary was joined by officers from all over Scotland and England, and Margaret Thatcher herself declared that the central government was going to help with the finances regarding the investigation.

About a week after the explosion, investigation had revealed that there were high traces of explosives, and this led the investigators to believe that an improvised explosive device (IED) had been used to destroy the plane. The FBI and many international investigators were inspecting the crash site, and they managed to recover around four million pieces of the plane. They were told to pick up anything that was not growing or was not a rock. They were instructed to inspect every single blade of grass and they interviewed around 10,000 people from numerous countries. Some of the countries that participated in the investigation were Austria, Germany, America, Switzerland, Great Britain, etc.

Thermographic cameras attached to helicopters were used to investigate the surrounding areas that were heavily wooded, and anything that was found was sent to a local school where it was checked through a gas chromatograph to learn whether there was any explosive residue on it.

The parts of the plane that were recovered were sent to a hanger in North West England where they were examined by Britain's Air Accidents Investigation Branch (AAIB). They found that the fuselage skin had been damaged and was torn back in a pattern that was indicative of an explosion. Britain's AAIB proposed some theories to determine the position and the quantity of the explosives used. Two suitcases were found -- AVN7511 and AVE4041 -- which showed some unusual characteristics. They showed some damage that left the investigators perplexed and confused for a moment. They realized that the suitcase AVE4041 had been placed close to the area where the explosion had taken place, and they noticed that the suitcase, because there was no blackening or soot on the floor of the container, but rather around it, was placed on top of another suitcase. There was no evidence at the time that proved that the bomb was placed inside this suitcase, but tests were soon carried out that confirmed the position and the quantity of the explosives used.

Suspects

Soon after the bombing, many sinister organizations tried to take responsibility for such a heinous act, but in the end, two Libyans were the main suspects for committing this wretched act of terror. Abdelbeset Ali Mohmed al Megrahi and Al Amin Khalifah Fhimah were charged and tried; however, the former Libyan was found guilty but not the latter.

Abdelbeset was a Libyan intelligence officer and head of security of Libyan Arab Airlines. Megrahi was convicted of murder and sentenced to imprisonment for life. However, after serving 10 years of his sentence, he was released on compassionate grounds on August 20, 2009.

Credit: the FBI

Thank you very much for buying this book. It really is very much appreciated. Please take a moment to write a brief review if you purchased it online.

Blessings, RJ Parker

Top Cases of The FBI – Volume 1

One of the most fascinating law enforcement agencies in the world is the FBI. From the J. Edgar Hoover days to the present, the Bureau has investigated the most famous cases, including mobsters, gangs, bank robbers, and terrorism. They have also received a few black eyes including the Waco Siege and Ruby Ridge.

From the Roaring Twenties to modern days, RJ Parker has written the true life events of cases that made major headlines all over the country. Each chapter in this book, is devoted to the biography (or background) of famous mobsters and horrendous events that the FBI has handled since the beginning of the agency.

These cases include:

John Dillinger and his gang of bank robbers
Mobster John Gotti
Bonnie and Clyde
Mobster Al Capone
The Jonestown Massacre
Oklahoma City Bombing
The Unabomber
The 1986 FBI Miami Shootout (In the Line of Fire)
Ruby Ridge
Waco
Patty Hearst
The D.C. Beltway Snipers

Amazon Kindle

Paperback

Audiobook

About the Author

RJ Parker, PhD, is an award-winning and bestselling true crime author and owner of RJ Parker Publishing, Inc. He has written over 30 true crime books which are available in eBook, paperback and audiobook editions and have sold in over 100 countries. He holds certifications in Serial Crime, Criminal Profiling and a PhD in Criminology.

To date, RJ has donated over 3,000 autographed books to allied troops serving overseas and to our wounded warriors recovering in Naval and Army hospitals all over the world. He also donates to Victims of Violent Crimes Canada.

If you are a police officer, firefighter, paramedic or serve in the military, active or retired, RJ gives his eBooks freely in appreciation for your service.

Contact Information

Bookbub:

rjpp.ca/BOOKBUB-RJPARKER

Author's Email:

AuthorRJParker@gmail.com

Publisher's Email:

Agent@RJParkerPublishing.com

Website:

http://m.RJPARKERPUBLISHING.com/

Twitter:

http://www.Twitter.com/realRJParker

Facebook:

https://www.facebook.com/RJParkerPublishing

Amazon Author's Page:

rjpp.ca/RJ-PARKER-BOOKS

The Basement

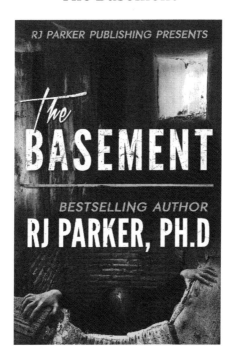

On March 24, 1987, the Philadelphia Police Department received a phone call from a woman who stated that she had been held captive for the last four months. When police officers arrived at the pay phone from which the call was made, Josefina Rivera told them that she and three other women had been held captive in a basement by a man named Gary Heidnik. This is a shocking story of kidnapping, rape, torture, mutilation, dismemberment, decapitation, and murder.

The subject matter in this book is graphic

http://rjpp.ca/THE-BASEMENT

Available in eBook, Paperback and Audiobook editions

Serial Killers Encyclopedia

The ultimate reference for anyone compelled by the pathology and twisted minds behind the most disturbing of homicidal monsters. From A to Z, and from around the world, these serial killers have killed in excess of 3,000 innocent victims, affecting thousands of friends and family members. There are monsters in this book that you may not have heard of, but you won't forget them after reading their case. This reference book will make a great collection for true crime aficionados.

WARNING: There are 15 dramatic crime scene photos in this book that some may find extremely disturbing.

http://bit.ly/SK-ENCYCLOPEDIA

Available in eBook, Paperback and Audiobook editions

Parents Who Killed Their Children

What could possibly incite parents to kill their own children?

This collection of "filicidal killers" provides a gripping overview of how things can go horribly wrong in once-loving families. Parents Who Killed Their Children depicts ten of the most notorious and horrific cases of homicidal parental units out of control. People like Andrea Yates, Diane Downs, Susan Smith, and Jeffrey MacDonald who received a great deal of media attention. The author explores the reasons, from addiction to postpartum psychosis, insanity to altruism.

Each story is detailed with background information on the parents, the murder scenes, trials, sentencing and aftermath.

http://bit.ly/PARENTSWHOKILLED

Available in eBook, Paperback and Audiobook editions

Blood Money: The Method and Madness of Assassins

From the old days of mobsters in smoky barrooms plotting to gun down their rivals, to the new age of ordinary people hiring contract killers through the Dark Web, this book depicts the history of assassins and how they work.

While movies portray assassins as glamorous, wealthy and full of mystery, the sober truth is often quite different.

The number of homicides credited to contract killers each year is staggering, and on the rise: business people killing their rivals, organized gang war kills, honor killings and even cold-blooded kills between spouses.

In *Blood Money: The Method and Madness of Assassins*, RJ Parker documents over a dozen infamous cases of professional assassins including Richard Kuklinski (The Ice Man), Charles Harrelson (Natural Born Killer) and Vincent Coll (Mad Dog).

Blood Money

Available in eBook, Paperback and Audiobook editions

References

Ciccarello, N.J., & Thompson, T.J. (2002). Money, the Fear of Failure, and Espionage: Report of an Interview with Robert Philip Hanssen. Langley, VA. *Personnel Security Managers' Research Program*.

Kelley, B.J. (2008). The Movie Breach: A Personal Perspective. *Studies in Intelligence*, *52*(1), 21-25.

Smith, I.C. (2004). Inside: A Top G-Man Exposes Spies, Lies, and Bureaucratic Bungling Inside the the FBI. Nashville, TN. *Nelson Current*, 301.

U.S. Department of Justice. (2003). A Review of the the FBI's Performance in Deterring, Detecting, and Investigating the Espionage Activities of Robert Philip Hanssen.

US Department of Justice. (2002). Commission for Review of the FBI Security Programs (Webster Commission). *A Review of the FBI Security Programs*.

FBI (n.d.). Brink's Robbery. Retrieved from https://www.fbi.gov/history/famous-cases/brinks-robbery

McFadden, R. (1981). Brink's Hold-up Spurs U.S. Inquiry on Links among Terrorist Groups. *NY Times*.

Sawyer, K. (1982). Police Push to Flush Out the Underground" Washington Post. *Washington Post*.

Schorow, S. (n.d.). The Crime of the Century: How the Brink's Robbers Stole Millions and the Hearts of Boston.Retrievedfrom http://www.stephanieschorow.com/the_crime_of_the_cen tury__how_the_brink_s_robbers_stole_millions_and_the_he arts__67354.htm

Steinhoff, P.G., & Zwerman, G. (n.d.). Accidents: Missing Mechanism or Challenge to the Model?

Wallis, C. (2011). A Widening Dragnet Surrounds Radical Underground. *Time Magazine*.

FBI (n.d.). Mississippi Burning. Retrieved from https://www.fbi.gov/history/famous-cases/mississippi-burning

Montaldo, C. (2017). The Mississippi Burning Case. Retrieved from https://www.thoughtco.com/the-mississippi-burning-case-972177

U.S. Department Of Justice. (n.d.). Investigation of the 1964 Murders of Michael Schwerner, James Chaney, and Andrew Goodman. *U.S. Department of Justice, Civil Rights Division*.

Biography.com. (2014). Donnie Brasco Law Enforcement (1939–). Retrieved from

https://www.biography.com/people/donnie-brasco-17172110

FBI. (n.d.). Joe Pistone, Undercover Agent. Retrieved from https://www.fbi.gov/history/famous-cases/joe-pistone-undercover-agent

Mafia Wiki. (n.d.). Joseph D. Pistone. Retrieved from http://mafia.wikia.com/wiki/Joseph_D._Pistone

OSIA. (2005). Italian-American Crime Fighters: A Brief Survey. *The Order Sons of Italy in America*.

Anti-Defamation League. (2016). Tattered Robes: The State of the Ku Klux Klan in the United States.

Davis, R. (2016). 12 Horrific Crimes Committed By the KKK between 1921 and 2016. Retrieved from http://www.essence.com/culture/horrific-kkk-crimes

FBI (n.d.). KKK Series. Retrieved from https://www.fbi.gov/history/famous-cases/kkk-series

Pearl, C. (n.d.). The Start of the Ku Klux Klan. *EdHelper*.

Biography.com. (n.d.). Black Dahlia Biography.com (1924–c. 1947). Retrieved from https://www.biography.com/people/black-dahlia-21117617

Karadjis, S. (2014). The Murder of the Black Dahlia: The Ultimate Cold Case. Retrieved from http://www.crimemagazine.com/murder-black-dahlia-ultimate-cold-case

Taylor, T. (n.d.). Who Killed The Black Dahlia? The Tragic Life & Death of Elizabeth Short. Retrieved from https://www.prairieghosts.com/beth.html

The Time. (n.d.). The Black Dahlia. Retrieved from http://content.time.com/time/specials/packages/article/0,28804,1867198_1867170_1867291,00.html

Alex Gibney. (2005). Enron: The smartest guys in the room. Documentary. Magnolia Pictures.

Doran, James (2004-05-14). Enron Staff wins $85m, The Times, 2012-12-01.

Gravelle, J. CRS Report RL31551, Employer Stock in Pension Plans: Economic and Tax Issues.

Healy, Paul M. Krishna G. Palepu. (2003), The Fall of Enron. Journal of Economic Perspectives.

Jickling, M. (2003). The Enron Collapse: An Overview of Financial Issues. *CRS Report for Congress*.

Pavel, T., & Encontro, M. (2012). The Enron scandal. The *Chalmers University of Technology*.

Purcell, P. CRS Report RL31507, Employer Stock in Retirement Plans: Investment Risk and Retirement Security (7-7571).

Shorter, G. CRS Report RL31348, Enron and Stock Analyst Objectivity.

Alpert, B. (2015). Katrina brought billions of dollars -- and quite a bit of fraud. Retrieved from http://www.no-la.com/katrina/index.ssf/2015/08/katrina_brought_good_and_evil.html

The Associated Press (NBC). (2007). U.S.: Katrina aid fraud nears $500 million. Retrieved from http://www.nbc-news.com/id/22102213/ns/us_news-life/t/us-katrina-aid-fraud-nears-million/

Coenen, T. L. (2006). Financial Statement Fraud in the Katrina Aftermath. Retrieved from https://www.acfe.com/article.aspx?id=4294967617

Emergency Management. (2008). Hurricane Katrina Fraud Task Force Brings Storm of Justice.

Retrieved from

http://www.govtech.com/em/disaster/Hurricane-Katrina-Fraud-Task.html

FBI. (2008). More Than 900 Defendants Charged with Disaster-Related Fraud by Hurricane Katrina Fraud Task Force During Three Years in Operation.

Retrieved from

https://archives.fbi.gov/archives/news/pressrel/press-releases/more-than-900-defendants-charged-with-disaster-related-fraud-by-hurricane-katrina-fraud-task-force-during-three-years-in-operation

CNN (2013). Anthrax Fast Facts. Retrieved from http://edition.cnn.com/2013/08/23/health/anthrax-fast-facts/index.html

NPR (2011). Timeline: How The Anthrax Terror Unfolded. Retrieved from http://www.npr.org/2011/02/15/93170200/timeline-how-the-anthrax-terror-unfolded

The United States Department of Justice. (2010). Amerithrax Investigative Summary.

Greenspan, J. (1998). Remembering the 1988 Lockerbie Bombing. Retrieved from http://www.history.com/news/remembering-the-1988-lockerbie-bombing

McCulloch, T. (1990). Presentation of Detective Chief Superintendent Tom McCulloch. Lockerbie Investigation for AVSEC World.

The opinion of the court delivered by the Lord Justice General in appeal against conviction of Abdelbaset Ali Mohmed Al Megrahi (Appellant) against Her Majesty's Advocate (Respondent): Appeal No C104/01 14. 2002. Retrieved from: http://www.bintulu.org/news/2009/08/22/libya-britaian-gaddafi-hugslockerbie-bomber.php.

Rosenberg, J. (2017). The bombing of Pan Am Flight 103 over Lockerbie. Retrieved from https://www.thoughtco.com/bombing-of-pan-am-flight-103-1779398

Ushynskyi, S. (2009). Pan Am flight 103 investigation and lessons learned. Aviation, 13(3), 78-86

Aftergood, S. (2015). Soviet Spy Ronald W. Pelton to be released from Prison. Retrieved from https://fas.org/blogs/secrecy/2015/11/pelton-release/

Cornwell, R. (2014). John Walker: American naval officer who formed a family spy ring that passed highly damaging secrets to the Soviet Union. Retrieved from http://www.independent.co.uk/news/obituaries/john-walker-american-naval-officer-who-formed-a-family-spy-ring-that-passed-highly-damaging-secrets-9704890.html

Engelberg, S. (1985). Officials Think Spying Led To Death Of C.I.A. Informant In Ghana. Retrieved from http://www.nytimes.com/1985/07/13/us/officials-think-spying-led-to-death-of-cia-informant-in-ghana.html

Mattingly, D. (2015). 1985 Jonathan Pollard: The Year of the Spy. Retrieved from https://medium.com/the-spyglass/1985-jonathan-pollard-the-year-of-the-spy-d29e5271f146

May, L. (1986). Pelton Gets Three Life Terms for Spying. Retrieved from http://articles.latimes.com/1986-12-17/news/mn-3283_1_three-life-terms

PBS. (n.d.). Four Chinese Espionage Investigations. Retrieved from http://www.pbs.org/wgbh/pages/frontline/shows/spy/spies/four.html

Rosenzweig, D. (2002). Engineer Sentenced in Nuclear Trigger Case. Retrieved from http://articles.latimes.com/2002/apr/30/local/me-krytron30

Biography.com Editor. (2014). Machine Gun Kelly. Retrieved from https://www.biography.com/people/machine-gun-kelly-507610

OceanView Publishing. (n.d.). George "Machine Gun" Kelly. Retrieved from http://www.alcatrazhistory.com/mgk.htm

Walsh, R. (2016). George 'Machine Gun' Kelly. Retrieved from http://swordandscale.com/george-machine-gun-kelly/

Made in the USA
Lexington, KY
03 May 2018